HEBREWS

1 AND 2 PETER;

1, 2, 3 JOHN; JUDE

STUDENT

GENESIS TO REVELATION SERIES

BOOK 23

Scripture quotations in this publication, unless otherwise indicated, are taken from the HOLY BIBLE, NEW INTERNATIONAL VERSION®. Copyright © 1973, 1978, 1984 International Bible Society. Used by permission of Zondervan Bible Publishers. All rights reserved.

ISBN 978-0-687-06236-2

Manufactured in the United States of America

11 – 18 17 16

ABINGDON PRESS

Nashville

About the Writer

Dr. Keith Schoville is chairman of the Department of Hebrew and Semitic Studies, University of Wisconsin, Madison, Wisconsin.

TABLE OF CONTENTS

In these last days [God] has spoken to us by his Son (1:2).

1

Jesus, God's Superior Messenger

Hebrews 1:1–4:13

DIMENSION ONE:
WHAT DOES THE BIBLE SAY?

Answer these questions by reading Hebrews 1

1. List the characteristics that set God's Son above the prophets (1:2-3)

2. How is the Son superior to the angels? (1:6-7, 14)

3. Why was the Son anointed above all his companions? (1:9)

Answer these questions by reading Hebrews 2

4. In 2:1, the reader is warned of the danger of drifting away. What is the reader warned of in 2:3a?

5. Identify the three sources that testify to the "great salvation" provided in Christ. (2:3b-4)

6. Why was the Son, who is superior to the angels, made lower than the angels for a time? (2:9)

7. The writer of Hebrews emphasizes the human experience of the Lord (2:14-18). What specific human experiences of his are mentioned in this section?

Answer these questions by reading Hebrews 3

8. Jesus and Moses are both described as faithful to God in 3:1-6. What phrases indicate Moses' relationship to God and the superior relationship of Christ to God? (3:5-6)

9. In 3:7-19, three dangers are listed: never entering God's rest, falling away from the living God, and the possibility of not sharing in Christ. What is the basic cause for these disasters? (3:12, 19)

10. What can be done to safeguard the believer from the sin's deceitfulness? (3:13)

11. In the previous section, failure to enter into God's rest was the result of unbelief. In 4:1-13, a different but equivalent word is used. What is that word? (4:11)

Answer this question by reading Hebrews 4:1-13

12. Why is it impossible to hide disobedience or unbelief from God? (4:12-13)

DIMENSION TWO:
WHAT DOES THE BIBLE MEAN?

We do not know exactly who wrote the Letter to the Hebrews, but clearly the first readers were Jewish Christians. The writer assumes that they are quite familiar with the Judaism of the first century.

Those first readers were in danger of casting off their faith that Jesus was the Messiah who had fulfilled the law of Moses. They apparently were tempted to return to Judaism, although they had not yet done so (6:9-12). Thus, the emphasis of the letter is on the superiority of Jesus Christ above everything connected with the earlier phase of biblical religion based on the law of Moses.

❏ *Hebrews 1:1-3.* Since he is going to focus on the superiority of Christ, the writer begins by emphasizing the ultimate nature of God's revelation in Christ. God spoke at various times in the past, in a number of different ways, by a variety of prophets. These prophets were servants who spoke only what God revealed to them. They prophesied over a considerable period of time, from Abraham's day, about 2000 B.C., until the time of Malachi, about 400 B.C. Each prophet spoke in his own peculiar style. The revelation came to the prophets sometimes in visions, sometimes through dreams, sometimes by a direct word from God.

By contrast, the writer of Hebrews says the Son has spoken "in these last days," in a ministry of less than four years. He was no servant with limited knowledge and experience of God, dependent on God for a communication from above, as were the prophets. Lines of direct communication were open between God and the Son. Jesus Christ is God's Son, the heir of all things. He is a messenger who reflects the glory of God, as Moses did when he came down from the holy mountain after talking with God (Exodus 34:29-35), but who also bears the very stamp of God's nature.

The Son not only created the world; the universe operates because of his powerful word. This Son, after he had completed his teaching, made purification of sins for humankind. The prophets were concerned with human failings and sin, but they could do nothing about this condition except to warn of God's displeasure and its consequences. By contrast, the Son was able to make purification for sins.

After the Son's atoning death, he sat down at the place of honor at God's right hand. The tombs and the bones of the prophets, however, remain here below.

❏ **Hebrews 1:4–2:18.** Hebrews 1:5-13 consists of seven quotations from the Old Testament that testify that the Son is superior to the angels.

- *5a from Psalm 2:7.* God designated Jesus as son and heir, but no angel was ever so designated. In the Gospel of Luke (3:22), a voice from heaven utters these words at the baptism of Jesus.
- *1:5b from 2 Samuel 7:14a.* This verse is part of God's promise to David through the prophet Nathan concerning a coming great king who would arise in David's line. The Old Testament views Solomon as the fulfillment of this promise. Here the application is made to the Son, who is later identified as Jesus (2:9).
- *1:6 from Deuteronomy 32:43* (Septuagint [Greek] version). This version was the Bible of most early Christians. In Deuteronomy, God is the object of worship. In the light of

the relationship of Father and Son described earlier, the Son becomes the object of worship here. Angels worship the Son, who is above them in relationship to God.

- *1:7 from Psalm 104:4.* God's creatures, the angels, are depicted as momentary messengers, like winds and flashes of lightning (the probable meaning of "flames of fire"). While the angels are extraordinary messengers of God, they're still servants.

- *1:8-9 from Psalm 45:6-7.* The psalm, referring to a king, is here applied to the Son. The point is the permanence of the Son in contrast to the brevity of angels (verse 7). As king, the Son is superior to his comrades because he is a king who loves righteousness and hates lawlessness, as an exceptional king will do.

- *1:10-12 from Psalm 102:25-27.* The psalm refers to God. Here the writer applies these verses to the Son. He emphasizes the permanence of the Son in contrast to the limited existence of God's creation, the heavens and the earth.

- *1:13 from Psalm 110:1.* The Son has been invited to sit at the right hand of God. Such an invitation was never extended to an angel. The favor of God has made it possible for the Son to rule free of the threat of enemies.

Having laid the groundwork, the writer of the letter exhorts his readers in 2:1-4. Since the Son is superior to the prophets and superior to the angels, those who hear his superior message should pay particular heed to it and not drift away. Although the Old Testament does not refer to God's use of angels in delivering the law to Moses at Mount Sinai, it was a tradition that is also alluded to in Acts 7:38. The question in 2:3, "How shall we escape if we ignore such a great salvation?" assumes the answer "We cannot!" The message delivered by angels was valid. The message of the Lord is founded on even more substantial witnesses: the word of the Lord, the testimony of the apostles, and the confirmation of God. That confirmation includes miraculous evidences and gifts of the Holy Spirit.

In 2:5-9, the writer continues to emphasize the superiority of Christ over the angels. The quotation in 2:6-8 is from Psalm 8. The point is that though humans are less than angels, God placed the world under human control, not under the control of angels. Humans have not been able to control everything; that control was lost through sin. Jesus is the true representative of humankind. Through him the control of all things is accomplished in order for this to be so, he had to "taste death for everyone" (2:9).

The idea of Jesus as the true (superior) human is expanded in 2:10-13. God is the source of the humanity of Jesus as well as our humanity. The one who can purify those who need purifying shared the common experience of being human. Thus it was appropriate that Jesus, through suffering and death, should pioneer the way by which countless individuals could come to share his glory. God is the source and cause of it all.

The suffering and death of Jesus, the perfect human, was extremely effective (2:14-18). In fact, it was a defeat for the devil, "who holds the power of death." People were shackled by the fear of death, but the death of Jesus and his triumph over the tomb freed them of this fear. He did this for those who have faith, the true descendants of Abraham. Further, Jesus' human experience, including death, made it possible for him to help people sympathetically in their afflictions. Since his death was sacrificial, he has become an effective high priest, able to atone for the sins of the people.

❏ *Hebrews 3:1-6.* Jesus was introduced in 2:17 as "a merciful and faithful high priest." By referring to Jesus as "apostle" (messenger), the writer draws our attention back to Jesus as God's superior revealer (2:3). The expression "God's house" refers to God's people Israel from Moses' time to Jesus and to the church. Jesus spoke of building his church on the bedrock of his being the Messiah (Matthew 16:18). In his letters the apostle Paul refers to the church as God's temple, another way of referring to the promised indwelling presence of the Holy Spirit in the believer.

The superiority of Jesus over Moses in relation to "God's house" is shown by these paired expressions:

Jesus	Moses
over God's house	in God's house
son	servant

❏ *Hebrews 3:7-19.* The quotation in 3:7-11 is from Psalm 95. The passage makes an example of those of Israel who did not enter the *rest,* that is, the Promised Land of Canaan, because they hardened their hearts in rebellion. The writer has in mind the rebellion that occurred when the Israelite explorers returned from exploring Canaan (Numbers 14:20-38). Out of that entire adult company, only Joshua and Caleb remained alive to enter the Promised Land.

The writer builds on this example in 3:12-19. An evil and unbelieving heart (3:12) can cause the same results "Today," that is, any time. The Israelites fell in the desert because they lost the " confidence they had at first" (3:14). Those who believe in Christ are urged to hold their first confidence firm to the end.

❏ *Hebrews 4:1-13.* The "rest" that the disobedient Israelites failed to gain was the Promised Land. Behind this expression, however, also stands the idea of the sabbath day, based on God's rest from creative activities on completing the formation of the cosmos (4:4). But neither the sabbath nor the land of Canaan are the sum total of God's rest. Psalm 95:11 speaks of entering God's rest in the future. Joshua's conquest of Canaan did not represent all God's rest (4:8-11). A future rest is yet to come for believers.

The land of Canaan became a model and forerunner of the eternal Promised Land. The "Sabbath-rest" that "remains" (4:9) is a heavenly rest. The work of God's people on earth will end, and they will participate in a heavenly sabbath rest.

The writer urges the readers of the letter to strive to enter the future rest. He warns of the danger of turning (away from the living God, as in 3:12) through the same sort of disobedience (4:11). Disobedience is the equivalent of unbelief (3:18-19).

No one can hide unbelief from God because the divine word penetrates the core of one's being. The "word of God" does not here refer to a book but to the revealing word, spoken through messengers: the prophets, the Son, the apostles. The thoughts and intentions of the heart are exposed to the One who will determine who shall enter the eternal rest. The reference is clearly to God.

DIMENSION THREE:
WHAT DOES THE BIBLE MEAN TO ME?

1. American culture has become more and more pluralistic in recent decades, with growing groups of Muslims, Buddhists, and Scientologists, for example. In light of this, how important to you is the claim of the superiority of Christ presented thus far in Hebrews? How important to your church is the superiority of Christ?

2. The writer of Hebrews was certain that his readers were in danger. The danger was that some of them might lose faith and turn away from God. What do you do to guard yourself from that danger? What would you recommend to others in the face of this danger?

3. Notice the phrase about the One "to whom we must give account" in Hebrews 4:13. How personal is the relationship you have with God? How can you become more aware of having to give account of yourself to Christ?

We have a great high priest who has gone through the heavens, Jesus the Son of God (4:14).

2

Jesus, God's Superior High Priest

Hebrews 4:14–7:28

DIMENSION ONE:
WHAT DOES THE BIBLE SAY?

Answer these questions by reading Hebrews 4:14–5:14.

1. Why should Christians expect to receive a sympathetic hearing at the throne of grace? (4:15)

2. What is the function of a high priest? (5:1)

3. Of what benefit to other people was the obedient suffering of Jesus? (5:8-9)

4. Why was the writer of Hebrews annoyed with those to whom he wrote? (5:11-14)

5. The "elementary teachings about Christ" are mentioned in 6:1. What are included in these teachings? (6:1-2)

6. To what spiritual blight does the writer compare culti-vated land that bears thorns and thistles? (6:4-8)

7. In what way does the faithful person show love for God? (6:10)

8. What has been the basis of hope for believers from Abra-ham to the time when Hebrews was written? (6:13-18)

Answer these questions by reading Hebrews 7

9. Why was the priesthood of Melchizedek considered end-less? (7:3)

10. In verse 7, the words *lesser* and *greater* are used. To whom do they refer? (7:4-7)

11. Why was the Levitical priesthood replaced by "the order of Melchizedek"? (7:11)

12. The priesthood of the tribe of Levi was established under the law of Moses. How is the priesthood of the Lord justified? (7:12-17)

13. What makes Jesus "the guarantee of a better covenant"? (7:20-22)

14. List the ways in which Jesus, as permanent priest, is superior to the former priesthood. (7:26-27)

DIMENSION TWO:
WHAT DOES THE BIBLE MEAN?

In our first lesson we learned that the writer of Hebrews stressed the superiority of Jesus as the revealer of God's message. In this lesson we turn our attention to the second major emphasis of the sermon/letter—Jesus is a superior high priest.

The priesthood under the law of Moses is somewhat strange to us because it operated in a period long before our time. We have no firsthand experience with it. Even if we were members of the early church, only those of us who had been Jewish would have an intimate relationship to the Levitical priesthood. Likely only a few of the first readers of Hebrews had actually attended the Temple services, since we assume that they were living somewhere outside Jerusalem.

Even if they never visited the Temple in Jerusalem, people living toward the end of the first century A.D. were well aware of temples and priests as a normal part of the religions of the day. Most knew of the Levitical priesthood too. They learned of it just as we do—from the descriptions of that priesthood in the Old Testament.

Understanding something of the priesthood that began with Aaron, Moses' brother, is important to the study of Hebrews. Our focus will be on the superior priesthood of Jesus, but the similarities to and differences from the Levitical priesthood are essential for appreciating Jesus as the ultimate high priest.

❏ *Hebrews 4:14-16.* Aaron, Moses' brother, was the first Israelite high priest. He was of the tribe of Levi, which is why we speak of the Levitical priesthood.

The writer emphasizes holding fast our confession because Jesus is "a great high priest." The Levitical high priest passed through the veil of the Temple into the Most Holy Place (Holy of Holies) once each year on the Day of Atonement, Jesus entered into heaven. He was the fulfillment of what the annual actions of the high priest only symbolized—humans becoming holy enough to enter God's holy presence.

Jesus was tempted, like all other high priests, but he did not sin. That is why he is so great and so able to provide mercy and grace.

❏ *Hebrews 5:1-10.* The purpose of a high priest was to act on behalf of the people before God. The high priest was to be holier than the people because he stood between the less holy people and the most holy God. Unlike Jesus, who was without sin, the Levitical high priest offered a sacrifice for his own sins as well as for the sins of the people. While there is this difference between them, Jesus and Aaron do share something else in common—each was called by God (5:4-5).

Our writer did not need to remind his readers of the call and appointment of Aaron. They were aware of the Old Testament passage that gives the account of his call and appointment (Leviticus 8). But the writer did want the readers to know the basis for Christ's call and appointment. So, in verse 5, he quotes Psalm 2:7 and in verse 6, Psalm 110:4.

Notice the phrase *the one who could save him from death* in verse 7. You will recall that in our first lesson we emphasized that the devil does not hold the ultimate power of life and death. This verse substantiates that God retains that power.

Jesus qualified for his high priestly office by learning obedience. Jesus prayed and was heard. His prayers were answered. He did not pray to escape the will of God for his life. (See his prayer in Gethsemane, Luke 22:42.) He sought strength to face whatever was necessary for the accomplishment of God's purposes in his life (and in his death).

The perfection of Jesus is the attainment of what he had the potential to be—the source of eternal salvation to all who obey him. We speak of something perfect when it has reached completion. Jesus did not complete his work, God's purpose for his life, until he breathed his last on the cross. With that perfection, God designated him a high priest. His high priesthood is after the order of Melchizedek, however, not after the order of Aaron. We will learn more of what this means later.

❑ *Hebrews 5:11–6:8.* That the writer of Hebrews is a preacher as well as a teacher is evident here. He has just referred to the priesthood of Jesus after the order of Melchizedek, and he plans to instruct his readers on the subject. But first he exhorts them to pay attention. They will be asked to think about the priesthood in ways they have not considered before. So, to stimulate their minds, he charges them with being slow to understand. They should be sharp, but they are dull.

The first readers of Hebrews should have been mature enough in their faith to teach the faith to others. Instead, they needed to be taught again "the elementary truths of God's word" (5:12). These first principles are expanded on in 6:1-3, where they are called "the elementary teachings about Christ."

The elementary teachings are the foundation of faith, not the end of it. Going on to maturity requires mental effort (5:14). Those who become mature in the faith think about what is good and what is bad and why.

What are the first principles? *Repentance* is a radical change in direction from past sinful deeds. *Faith* is trust in God's grace, rather than dependence on words. *Baptisms* and *laying on of hands* were practiced in Judaism. Christians also touched and prayed for individuals in connection with forgiveness of sins, healing, and the blessing of the Holy Spirit. The *resurrection of the dead* and *eternal judgment* were well-known ideas among the Jews of Jesus' time. The Lord gave deeper meanings to them by his own passion and resurrection.

The point of our writer is that the readers should leave these basics. They should give thought to more mature matters and come to understand the significance of the high priestly work of Jesus.

Continuing to be immature increases the danger of sliding into apostasy (6:4-8). Notice the words *impossible to be brought back*. With God, nothing shall be called impossible (Matthew 19:26). The only unforgivable sin is that sin unrepented and unconfessed.

The apostate cannot be renewed because of the hardening of the heart. Apostasy involves the denial of Jesus, the denial of the truth and validity of the gospel, and reaching a mental state beyond repentance. The state of the apostate is described as similar to cultivated land that not only produces nothing but, even worse, produces exactly the opposite of what the farmer would expect.

❏ *Hebrews 6:9-20.* The major danger of continuing in an immature state as a Christian is to fall away. The writer of Hebrews meant to do nothing more than arouse his readers to this danger. He did not charge them with that ultimate error. In fact, in 6:9-12, his exhortation takes on an encouraging note. Rather than slipping away from the effects of salvation in Jesus, they have given evidence of their sincere faith. They have been serving the saints. They have been meeting the needs of brothers and sisters in Christ who, we can assume, lacked the necessities of life as a result of the persecutions they endured.

His first concern is that they not be lazy Christians. If they are to inherit the promises (of God in Christ Jesus), they need faith and patience. They need to imitate people of faith and patience.

Abraham is an excellent example of one who, through faith and patience, "received what was promised" by God (6:13-15). Apart from patient endurance, however, he received the promise because God's promises are certain (6:16-18). God's promise to Abraham was based on two unchanging things: first, God's word of promise (certain because God does not lie) and second, God's oath sworn "by himself."

Notice the descriptive terms in 6:18-19: "We who have fled," like those who fled to the cities of refuge in Old Testament times (Deuteronomy 4:41-43; 19:1-10); "to take hold of the hope," an anchor for the soul. Absolute security is there, to keep the faithful from slipping away.

That hope is in Jesus who has entered into the inner sanctuary behind the curtain. Entering the inner sanctuary is an allusion to Christ's entry into heaven after his ascension. One enters God's presence in heaven. Entry into the presence of God is the destiny of the followers of Jesus. He is a forerunner on behalf of his followers.

❏ **Hebrews 7:1-28.** You may recall that the writer said he had much to say on the topic of the high priesthood "in the order of Melchizedek" (5:10-11). After his lengthy exhortation, he returns to the subject in 6:20. The proofs of the superiority of Jesus as high priest over the priesthood of Aaron follow.

Melchizedek was both a king and a priest. We meet him in Genesis 14:18-20. His name means the king of (*melchi*) righteousness (*zedek*) and indicates his character. Also, he was king of (Jeru) Salem, the city of peace (shalom). Aaron was only a priest.

The Bible contains no record of Melchizedek's birth or death. Nor is a family connection recorded (7:3). His priesthood is older than the Levitical priesthood; thus, his supersedes it and survives it. Abraham (and his descendants through him) paid tithes to Melchizedek, the priest of "the Most High God." Further, Melchizedek blessed Abraham—the lesser person being blessed by the greater. Thus, a priest after the order of Melchizedek is far greater than Abraham and his descendants, including Levi, Aaron, and the Levitical priesthood.

The priesthood after the order of Melchizedek is superior to the Levitical priesthood, too, because the Levitical priesthood was temporary and inadequate (7:11-19). The priesthood established as a part of the law of Moses was not able to perfect people. The sacrifices were repeated year after year after year. So, long after Moses and Aaron, God indicated that a permanent high priest would be appointed (Hebrews 7:17; Psalm 110:4). An appointment under the older, more permanent order meant that the temporary Levitical order would pass away.

The priestly order of Melchizedek could not be established under the law of Moses, for its regulations had to do only with the Levitical priesthood. A change in the law was also required. That change made possible the appointment of someone from a non-Levitical family as priest. Jesus, from the tribe of Judah, was that priest (7:11-14). His appointment is based on his indestructible life (7:16).

This priesthood of Jesus is superior to the Levitical priesthood in these ways:

1. he was confirmed in office by God's oath; the Levitical priests were not (7:20-21);

2. his is a permanent priesthood; theirs was limited to their length of life, after which another high priest was appointed (7:23-25);

3. he is perfect forever; they were sinners who had to offer sacrifices for their own sins as well as for the sins of the people (7:26-28).

Thus, with Jesus as high priest, we have a better hope (7:19), a better covenant (7:22), a permanent intercessor (7:25), and a perfect priest (7:28).

DIMENSION THREE:
WHAT DOES THE BIBLE MEAN TO ME?

1. How important is the advice in Hebrews on spiritual maturity and the danger of apostasy? How important is it to your church?

2. What can the reference to the prayer of Jesus (5:7-10) teach us about personal prayer and the corporate prayers of the church?

*We do have . . . a high priest, who sat down at
the right hand of the throne of the Majesty in heaven (8:1).*

—— 3 ——

Jesus, Priest of a Better Covenant, Tent, and Sacrifice

Hebrews 8:1–10:18

DIMENSION ONE:
WHAT DOES THE BIBLE SAY?

Answer these questions by reading Hebrews 8

1. Where is the high priest of Christians now located? (8:1b)

2. Moses constructed the earthly tabernacle after what pattern? (8:5)

3. Why is the new covenant, under which Christ has his ministry, better than the old covenant? (8:6)

4. How can we be certain that the first covenant was not faultless? (8:7)

5. With what people did the Lord promise to establish the new covenant? (8:8)

6. What did the Lord promise to do for his people under the new covenant? (8:10)

Answer these questions by reading Hebrews 9

7. What did the ark of the covenant contain? (9:4)

8. What did the high priest always carry with him when he entered the second (inner) room? (9:6-7)

9. How often did Christ enter into the "perfect tabernacle," and what did he take with him? (9:11-12)

10. What is the blood of Christ able to do? (9:14)

11. How did the old covenant make possible the forgiveness of sins? (9:22)

12. For whose benefit did Christ appear before God in heaven? (9:24)

13. For what purpose will Christ appear a second time? (9:28)

Answer these questions by reading Hebrews 10:1-18

14. What did Christ desire to do when he came into the world? (10:7)

15. Under the new covenant, what two things did the Lord promise to do? (10:16-17)

DIMENSION TWO:
WHAT DOES THE BIBLE MEAN?

As we study the passages of this lesson, notice that the writer continues to emphasize the superiority of the priesthood of Jesus. This basic idea is extended and enhanced by biblical quotations with which his first readers would have been familiar.

❏ *Hebrews 8:1-6.* This section introduces a comparison between Christ as minister in a superior, heavenly sanctuary and the Levitical priests as ministers in an earthly sanctuary. Notice the word *serves* (ministers) in 8:2 and *ministry* in 8:6. They tie the passage and the ideas together. Christ is not a high priest located on earth who functions in an earthly tabernacle.

The expression *such a high priest* refers to the last verse of Chapter 7. That verse mentions the Son, the perfect high priest, who is appointed a priest forever by God's oath. This high priest is the One who is seated at God's right hand.

Sat down at the right hand is an expression that implies honor, power, and a position of authority. Just as an earthly king might honor his first-born son by giving the son a seat next to his throne, so God has given the seat on his right hand to Christ.

Although seated on a throne at the right hand of God, Christ is said to *serve* by the writer of Hebrews. Here the word means "to serve (or minister) as priest." Christ serves in the "true tabernacle," that is, the sanctuary in heaven, rather than the Temple in Jerusalem or the earthly tabernacle. You will recall that the Temple was built on the plan of the earlier tabernacle. The Tabernacle was first built at the foot of the holy mountain in Sinai where Moses and the people of Israel met with God.

The Tabernacle in the desert was a copy of the heavenly original. That is the point of 8:5. The detailed plan for the Tabernacle was given to Moses by God, and it was patterned after the original in heaven. The heavenly original was "set up," that is built, by the Lord, not by humans. The earthly tabernacle was set up by humans, even though the plan was delivered from heaven.

Verses 3 and 4 refer to the offering of gifts and sacrifices. This is the ministry of priests. The Levitical priests have something to offer on earth. These are the gifts and sacrifices that the people of God bring to the Tabernacle. The sacrifices are specified in the law of Moses (Exodus 29:38-46; Leviticus 1–7).

Jesus could not be a priest when he was on earth. He was from a different tribe, so he could not fulfill the requirements for the Levitical priesthood under the old covenant. The priests offered gifts according to that law, and Christ, as the heavenly high priest, must also have something to offer (8:3). With this statement, our writer introduces the idea of the self-sacrifice of Jesus. But the subject will not be discussed further until Chapter 9.

In 8:5, we find the idea that the earthly sanctuary serves as "a copy and shadow" of the heavenly sanctuary. The "true tabernacle" is the original in heaven. Clearly the true tabernacle is better than the earthly "copy and shadow." So, Christ has a better priestly ministry in the original sanctuary in heaven than the Levitical priests had in the earthly copy, the Tabernacle (8:6).

Verse 6 introduces a related topic, that Christ is the high priest under a better covenant. This topic is the main emphasis of this section of Hebrews. Our writer assumes that everything related to the reconciling ministry of Jesus is superior to that of the old covenant—the priesthood, the sanctuary, the sacrifice, and the new covenant. Christ mediates the new and better covenant. This covenant is better than the old covenant given through Moses because it is established "on better promises."

❏ *Hebrews 8:7-13.* Our writer argues (8:7) that the enactment of the new covenant proves, first, that it was needed and, second, that the old covenant was faulty. The proof that the old covenant was faulty and would be replaced is based on the word of the Lord to the prophet Jeremiah (31:31-34). This quotation makes up 8:8-12.

We will examine the quotation in detail, but before we do, read the concluding remarks in 8:13. God has treated the covenant mediated through Moses as obsolete because God spoke through Jeremiah many centuries after he spoke through Moses.

Did God produce something imperfect when God gave the law to Moses on Mount Sinai? No, the law was perfectly suited to God's purposes, according to Paul. It was "put in charge to lead us to Christ" (Galatians 3:24). "The law is holy, and the commandment is holy, righteous and good" (Romans 7:12). But "all who rely on observing the law are under a curse, for it is written: 'Cursed be everyone who does not continue to do everything written in the Book of the Law.' Clearly no one can be justified before God by the law, because, 'The righteous will live by faith.' The law is not based on faith; on the contrary, 'The man who does these things will live by them' " (Galatians 3:10-12). By means of the commandment, the utterly sinful nature of sin was shown (Romans 7:13).

God did not find fault with the law but with his people. The phrase *the people* (8:8) refers to the generation after generation of Israelites who failed to keep the commandments of the old covenant. The destruction of the Northern Kingdom (Israel) by the Assyrians in 721 B.C. and their captivity was the consequence of despising the law of the Lord (2 Kings 17:7-18). The conquest of the Southern Kingdom (Judah) by Nebuchadnezzar, king of Babylon, in the days of Jeremiah was also attributed to sin (Jeremiah 19:3-9). As God noted through Jeremiah, God turned away from them because they "did not remain faithful to my covenant" (Hebrews 8:9). So a new covenant was promised even as they were going into captivity (8:8-9).

Just as God took the initiative to establish the old covenant (8:9), so God would establish a new covenant at some undetermined time in the future. The new covenant was not established as the basis for life when the Jews returned to rebuild Jerusalem after the "seventy years" of exile prophesied by Jeremiah (25:12). The law of Moses was the basis for the renewal of life and worship among the Jews. The new covenant was established by Jesus. Paul reports these words of Jesus spoken at the Last Supper: "This cup is the new covenant in my blood" (1 Corinthians 11:25).

The main points of the new covenant are given here (8:10-12):

1. God's laws will be impressed on the hearts and minds of God's people, rather than on tablets of stone. A new power to know and to obey God's will is the result.

2. God will identify with God's people, and God's people will identify with God. An intimacy will exist between the Creator and the created that was not experienced under the old covenant.

3. All God's people will experience God. To know the Lord is to have a direct experience of God. Under the new covenant, simply being born and being taught does not make one a child of God. The new birth must be experienced (John 3:5). To experience the new birth is to receive the indwelling presence of the Holy Spirit, and the Lord is the Spirit (2 Corinthians 3:17-18). No one can teach this personal involvement with God. It must be experienced.

4. God will be merciful, forgiving and forgetting sins. Under the old covenant, the sins of each year were remembered on the Day of Atonement.

These are the better promises of the new covenant.

❏ *Hebrews 9:1-14.* The first covenant and the plans for the earthly sanctuary were both given at the same time, when Moses conferred with God on the holy mountain. The law of Moses included the regulations for worship (9:1).

Under the law, the outer Tabernacle, "the Holy Place," contained the furnishings listed in 9:2. A curtain probably separated the Holy Place from the outer court. The inner (part of the) tabernacle, behind another curtain, was "the Most Holy Place," or "Holy of Holies."

Within the Most Holy Place were a golden altar of incense and the ark of the covenant. The three items in the ark were remaining evidences of God's grace, goodness, and power shown to his people in the past. Aaron's staff was a reminder of the Exodus (Numbers 13:1-11). The jar of manna was a reminder of God's provision for the Israelites in the desert (Exodus 16:31-35). The tablets of the covenant, containing the Ten Commandments, were a reminder of God's agreement to be the people's God under the provisions to which they agreed (Exodus 24:3-8).

The cherubim (9:5) were golden figures, representing the angelic host serving God about the heavenly throne. The cherubim were affixed to the lid of the ark, which was called the mercy seat.

All these items were filled with symbolism in the mind of the writer, but to explain them would take time and divert him from his focus. So he proceeded with that focus.

Having described the layout of the earthly tabernacle, its use is noted (9:6-7). The Holy Place was entered regularly by the priests in their duties. The New Testament records, for example, Zechariah, the father of John the Baptist, engaged in serving in the Holy Place (Luke 1:8-23). The ministry of the high priest in the Most Holy Place is noted next (Hebrews 9:7).

The Tabernacle/Temple and its continuing ministries indicate that the way into the true sanctuary, heaven itself, was not yet opened. The sacrifices could not really cleanse the conscience of the worshiper in preparation for standing in the presence of the holy God. A veil of separation remained between God and the worshiper. The sacrifices and cleansing rituals were limited in effectiveness for the worshiper. They were also limited in time, until "the time of the new order" (9:10). Behind this expression is the idea that the present evil age will be ended by God and a new age will begin. In that time God will give all that God has promised. Just as the old covenant is becoming obsolete and is ready to vanish (8:13), so its related sanctuary and priestly ministry are to give way to the new and better way.

Christ has appeared as the superior high priest. What this means for believers is spelled out in 9:11-14. "The good things that are already here" (9:11) must refer to the "new order" mentioned just above. The superior priest has entered the Holy Place of heaven, not with the blood of animals, but with his own blood. He was an acceptable sacrifice, without spot or blemish; and his blood is able to do what the blood of innocent animals could not do—cleanse the conscience. The cleansing is from dead works. These are likely the useless rituals of the old sanctuary that could not "clear the conscience of the worshiper" (9:9b). The purpose of the purification is in preparation to serve the living God.

❑ *Hebrews 9:15-28.* Not only is Christ a superior high priest and his blood a more powerful sacrifice, that blood also validates the new covenant. Under the new covenant, "those who are called" (9:15) are able to receive the promised inheritance. (Recall that the generation in the desert was not able to enter the promised [earthly] inheritance [Hebrews 3:16-19].) The called are those who have responded to the gospel invitation to be confirmed to the image of God's Son (Romans 8:29-30).

The sacrificial death of Jesus made the receiving of the promised eternal inheritance possible because

1. the called have been set free from the penalty of the sins committed under the old covenant (9:15);

2. the will (new covenant) became effective at his death (9:16-17).

The first covenant, with poorer promises than the new covenant, was made valid with the death of a sacrificial animal (Exodus 24:3-8). That blood was a symbol of the validation of the covenant God proposed and the people accepted. The blood was sprinkled on the people and on the book containing God's covenant agreement. Similarly, Moses purified the tabernacle sanctuary and everything related to it with blood (Leviticus 8:14-15, 30). Hebrews 9:22 states that "without the shedding of blood there is no forgiveness." Either the soul that sins shall die, or an acceptable substitute must die.

The sacrifice of animals as substitutes for Israelites and the purifying of the Tabernacle by animal blood were both satisfactory rituals for the earthly things. But the heavenly, spiritual realities required better sacrifices (9:23-24). Christ met all the requirements. Christ has entered the presence of God on our behalf. Christ died for sinners.

In the earthly sanctuary under the old covenant, the priests offered continual and annual sacrifices. Christ's sacrifice was sufficient once and for all. He offered himself at the end of the era of the old covenant to put away sin permanently (9:25-26).

The last verses of Hebrews 9 (27-28) offer an analogy intended to point to the difference between the death of Christ and that of others. "Man is destined to die once, and after that to face judgment." One exception to this rule is Christ. He bore the sins of many in his death, but because he was innocent, he did not face judgment. Rather, Christ entered heaven and is seated "at the right hand of the throne of the Majesty in heaven" (8:1). When Christ appears the second time, it will not be to deal with the problem of sin. He did that the first time. He will come again to save the called who are eagerly waiting for his appearing. The covenant he mediated has better promises.

❑ *Hebrews 10:1-10.* The writer has introduced the readers to the once-and-for-all character of Christ's self-sacrifice in 9:25-28. Now he expands that point. The new covenant is the reality of good things of which the law was just a shadow. The continual offering of animal sacrifices under the law never took away sin. Sin was remembered under that system. God used that shadow to anticipate something superior.

Using Psalm 40:6-8, the writer establishes that the superior sacrifice of Christ was essentially to do the will of God (10:5-7). God's will was to abolish the first (system of sacrifices under the old covenant) in order to establish the second (10:9b). The second is the offering of the body of Jesus Christ as a one-time, all-sufficient sacrifice (10:10). Both the writer and the readers of Hebrews are made holy through that sacrifice.

❑ *Hebrews 10:11-18.* In the earthly sanctuary, a shadow of the heavenly reality, priests stand as they perform the continual, repeated service. Christ's single, permanent sacrifice for sin has been offered. He has sat down at the right hand of God. His work is completed. All that remains is

1. that his enemies recognize and submit to his authority;

2. that the number of those who are sanctified be completed.

That Christ has completed his redeeming work is confirmed by the Holy Spirit through the words of Jeremiah.

The quotations are a part of the longer passage quoted earlier in 8:8-12. Verse 18 summarizes the sufficiency of Christ's redeeming work that is now finished. No more animal offerings for sin are necessary. The Day of Atonement is no longer needed. The problem of sin is solved. It is finished.

DIMENSION THREE:
WHAT DOES THE BIBLE MEAN TO ME?

1. Some people prefer to think about the love of Jesus and to ignore the blood of Jesus (Hebrews 9:22-26). How important is the doctrine of the blood atonement of Jesus to you? How important is this doctrine to the church?

2. Several expressions in our lesson refer to those who read Hebrews: *those whose consciences are cleansed* (9:14), *the called* (9:15), *those waiting for him* (9:28), and *those made holy* (10:10, 14). How do you think about yourself in relation to these expressions?

*Faith is being sure of what we hope for
and certain of what we do not see (11:1).*

—— 4 ——

Faith, the Superior Way to Do God's Will

Hebrews 10:19–11:40

DIMENSION ONE:
WHAT DOES THE BIBLE SAY?

Answer these questions by reading Hebrews 10:19-39

1. In 10:19-25, five exhortations begin with the words *let us*. What three actions does the writer call for?

2. Who should fear falling "into the hands of the living God"? (10:29, 31)

3. List the sufferings that early believers in Christ endured. (10:32-34)

4. Who are the opposite of "those who believe and are saved"? (10:39)

5. According to the writer of Hebrews, how can we under-stand the creation of the visible universe out of things that cannot be seen? (11:3)

6. List the patriarchs given as examples of faith in 11:4-7.

7. What did Abraham and Sarah have faith in? (11:8-13)

8. What is the common feature of the faith of Abraham, Isaac, Jacob, and Joseph? (11:17-22)

9. List the three things that Moses did by faith. (11:23-28)

10. Identify the two historical events that illustrate the faith of the Israelites. (11:29-30)

11. The accomplishments of God's judges and prophets are listed in 11:32-38. How were these great deeds done?

12. The heroic figures of faith mentioned in Hebrews 11 did not receive in their time what was promised. Why not? (11:39-40)

DIMENSION TWO:
WHAT DOES THE BIBLE MEAN?

The writer of Hebrews has presented two main points in the book: that Jesus is the supreme messenger of God and that Jesus is the ultimate high priest. He has established the truth of these facts on the basis of Scripture. Now, all that remains is for him to urge the readers to act on the evidence.

The remainder of the book consists of a lengthy exhortation to faith and perseverance and a shorter series of exhortations that closes the book.

❏ *Hebrews 10:19-25.* The main thought of this passage is in 10:22: "Let us draw near." The preceding verses set the stage for this exhortation. The readers can draw near confidently because Jesus opened the way into the sanctuary for those who are sanctified, made holy (10:14). The sanctuary is the presence of God in heaven (9:24).

Previously, nearness to the Most Holy Place was restricted more and more the nearer one drew toward the inner sanctum of the Tabernacle. No Gentile could enter the courts within the enclosure walls. Ritually clean Israelites could enter the courts, along with the priests; but only the priests could enter the Holy Place. Access to the Most Holy Place was restricted to the high priest, the most ritually pure person in Israel. Now, all those purified by the blood of Christ are holy enough to enter the presence of God.

The Christian has another reason to approach God confidently—the One who sanctifies is also the great high priest. Earlier we learned that the great high priest is seated at the right hand of the Majesty in heaven. His cleansing and his presence at God's right hand are the basis for confidently drawing near.

Those who draw near are expected to have these characteristics: their total beings (hearts, consciences, and bodies) have been made pure by the blood of Christ (9:14) and by baptism.

The readers are urged to have confidence and to "hold unswervingly to the hope we profess." The hope is in the promises of God. The confession is the verbal statement of that hope. Scripture testifies that believers are to "always be prepared to give an answer to everyone who asks you to give the reason for the hope that you have" (1 Peter 3:15b).

Because of this confidence, the readers also are urged to meet one another's needs lovingly. Participation in the community of the sanctified is urged (10:25). Mutual encouragement helps maintain one another's faith. The day of the Lord, when the content of the faith will be realized, is approaching.

❑ *Hebrews 10:26-31.* Those who neglect to meet together and to encourage one another may be flirting with the danger of deliberate sin, the sin of apostasy. No second sacrifice can remove such sin, for Jesus suffered once and for all time. That sacrifice, which alone is able to cleanse the conscience, cannot be repeated. Judgment will surely follow such sin. Just as everything connected with the old covenant was inferior to the new, the punishment under the new covenant for deliberate sin will be more fearful. Under the law of Moses, a deliberate sinner died without mercy at the hands of other human beings. Under the new covenant, the apostate will "fall into the hands of the living God."

❑ *Hebrews 10:32-39.* At the beginning of this exhortation, the writer encourages the readers confidently to draw near to the Lord. He also calls for them to encourage one another and warns them to be wary of falling into apostasy. After stressing that negative idea, he turns to a more positive emphasis.

The writer urges his readers to remember the former days. Those were the days of their conversion to Christ and the early period of their discipleship. What was that time in their lives like?

First, they "received the light." They were "called . . . out of darkness into his wonderful light" (1 Peter 2:9). The light of a sin-darkened world is Jesus. When through faith the light shines into the heart and mind of an individual, a new perspective on life results. Life begins to make sense.

Second, they endured public insults and persecution and shared the sufferings of other believers. By so doing, they followed the teaching of Jesus to visit those in prison (Matthew 25:36). The visits were to provide the necessities of life to the prisoners. Providing these necessities might be the meaning of accepting joyfully the plundering of property. The other possibility is that their property was confiscated by the government, and they counted it all joy to suffer on behalf of Christ.

Individual possessions are of little consequence to a member of Christ's kingdom. Jesus taught his disciples not to be anxious about their life, saying, " 'What shall we eat?' or 'What shall we drink?' or 'What shall we wear?' " (Matthew 6:25-34). Christians have a better, abiding possession—faith in God's promises. To lose this certainty is to risk losing the reward of faith.

Perseverance is needed. Certainty will help one persevere, and perseverance will provide the means to do the will of God and to receive what is promised.

To support his word, the writer quotes Habakkuk 2:3-4. The point in Hebrews 10:37-38 is that a righteous individual lives by faith, and God takes pleasure in that person. God, however, takes no pleasure in those who shrink back.

The last verse of Chapter 10 is a strong encouragement to the readers. Despite the strong warnings and exhortations that have been presented, the writer intends only to encourage the readers. He does not condemn them as being guilty of apostasy. Rather, he expresses his confidence that they are people of faith who will be saved.

❏ *Hebrews 11:1-3.* The writer has emphasized perseverance based on faith. Now faith itself becomes the focus. One part of faith is *being sure of.* Assurance combines hope, confidence, and trust. The focus of this assurance is "what we hope for." The other part of faith is *being certain of.* Certainty is conviction. The things hoped for are the things not seen. These are the promises of God. Faith is trusting God's word. This trust in God's word helps both the writer and the readers of Hebrews understand how the world came to be. God spoke, and it was so (Genesis 1).

❏ *Hebrews 11:4-7.* Genesis 4:1-16 tells the story of Cain and Abel. No direct statement there indicates why Abel's offering was accepted by God and Cain's was not. Our writer indicates that Abel's faith was the assurance and conviction that he was presenting his offering in the way God required. And it was accepted by God. Apparently Cain lacked confidence that he was acting acceptably before God.

Our text assumes that Cain did not offer his sacrifice in faith, while Abel did. The faith through which Abel still speaks is the testimony in God's Word.

We are told of Enoch that he "walked with God; then he was no more, because God took him away" (Genesis 5:24). In an apostate world Enoch trusted God and confidently walked with God. This pleased God. The reward of Enoch's faith was that he did not experience death. God took him away.

Noah was confident that God would fulfill God's promises. Noah believed a flood would come, so he acted on his faith in God's word. By his faith Noah saved his family. By it he also condemned the world. They scoffed at his faith, and they perished. Noah is called righteous in Genesis 7:1. He is the first person so designated in the Bible.

❏ *Hebrews 11:8-22.* Referring to Abraham, the writer of Hebrews repeats the phrase *by faith* three times in these verses. In 11:8, the phrase refers to God's call to Abraham to leave his native land to travel to a land he had never seen. God promised to give that land to him. In 11:9, Abraham is pictured as living in that promised land as a wandering stranger rather than the owner. He lived this way confident that God would honor his promises to him, even though he was not experiencing the full realization of those promises. In 11:17-19, the offering of Isaac by Abraham is recalled. When in that incident God tested his servant, Abraham trusted God. He trusted God even though the accomplishment of God's promises through the doomed Isaac looked impossible. Abraham was fully confident in each of these instances that what God had promised and what Abraham hoped for would come to pass.

Abraham's wife, Sarah, also provides an example of faith. She had confidence that God would accomplish what she hoped for, that she would be blessed with a son. Sarah was skeptical when she first heard that she would become pregnant (Genesis 18:9-15). Not only had she always been barren, she had reached the age when women are no longer fertile. Yet Sarah exhibited faith by having intercourse with her husband, and God gave her the power to conceive. Isaac, the son of promise, was the first of the descendants of Abraham. God had promised that Abraham's descendants would increase beyond number.

"These people" of 11:13 must refer to Abraham, Sarah, Isaac, Jacob, Joseph, and their families. They died, not having attained the promises, but confident of them. They had faith. We do not know how they visualized the "better country," heaven (11:16), but the writer of Hebrews is confident that they did.

Abraham once said to the Hittites, who lived in Canaan, the Promised Land: "I am an alien and a stranger among you" (Genesis 23:4). The reasoning of the writer of Hebrews is that if Abraham, while living in the Promised Land, still looked for "a better country" (Hebrews 11:16), that better country had to be heaven. Abraham's son and grandson continued to live as foreigners in the land of Canaan, so they must have shared his hope of a better country promised by God. That better country was actually a city (11:16). (The idea of heaven as a city is found also in Revelation 21.)

The assurance of the things Isaac, Jacob, and Joseph hoped for and their conviction of things not seen is fairly clear in 11:20-22. Joseph, before his death, ordered the Israelites to take his bones (mummy) with them when they left Egypt to return to Canaan, so he was confident of the fulfillment of God's promises there some time in the future.

❏ *Hebrews 11:23-31.* "By faith" is used four times of Moses, in 11:23, 24, 27, and 28. Verse 23 refers to the faith of his parents. They must have been convinced that this beautiful child would be blessed of God. Moses, when grown, rejected palace life for the greater promises of God. The assumption is that he learned of these promises at his mother's knee. As an example of a faithful servant of God, Moses suffered for the sake of the promises, even though he had not experienced their fulfillment.

Verse 27 probably refers to Moses' first departure from Egypt (Exodus 2:15), since it precedes the reference to the Passover. Moses endured because he was convinced of things not seen. His confidence was in God, "him who is invisible." The Passover looked to the very near future, yet it was the future based on the promise of God. Moses was confident God's promise about the destroyer passing over Egypt would be fulfilled. So by faith he followed the instructions about putting blood on the doorposts (Exodus 12:21-23).

The Israelites exhibited faith by crossing the divided sea (Exodus 14:21-31). They trusted God's word through Moses. Their faith also helped bring down the walls of Jericho. They had confidence in God's promises through Joshua. Even Rahab, the Canaanite woman, was saved by faith. She was convinced that God would enable the Israelites to conquer Canaan. Despite the dangers she might face from her neighbors in Jericho, Rahab acted in faith (Joshua 2:1-21; 6:22-25).

❏ *Hebrews 11:32-38.* This section is a summary of the faith of judges and prophets. A few of the heroes are named. We can read about their deeds in the books of Judges and First and Second Samuel. At first glance, Barak does not seem to be a good example of faith. He was only willing to lead the Israelites if Deborah would accompany him (Judges 4:1-10). Samson, too, seems to be an example of one who was full of passion for women rather than faithful to God (Judges 14–16). Yet, our writer sees their faith in the fact that Barak did conquer the Canaanites and Samson did pray and trust God to give him strength to avenge his enemies. "Thus he killed many more when he died than while he lived" (Judges 16:30c).

We do not know exactly who is intended by some of the references to deeds in 11:33-38. David might have been in the writer's mind in 11:33, except that Daniel shut the mouths of lions. Daniel's companions—Shadrach, Meshach, and Abednego—"quenched the fury of the flames" (Daniel 3). Some of the deeds are too general to associate with a particular person. A woman's son was revived by Elijah (1 Kings 17:8-24) and another by Elisha (2 Kings 4:8-37). Isaiah may have been the one "sawed in two" (Hebrews 11:37). Although the biblical texts do not state that Isaiah died by that means, it is an ancient tradition. The point of this long list is that those who were faithful over this long period of history suffered various persecutions, cruelties, and destitution for the sake of their faith.

❑ *Hebrews 11:39-40.* This long list of the faithful of the past is part of an exhortation to the readers. The writer is encouraging the readers to endure in their faith. He has paraded through their minds the faithful of the past. The reason for using the list is given in these two verses. Those faithful persons of the past died without receiving what their eyes of faith had seen, what God had promised. What they looked for was being fulfilled in the time of the writer and his first readers. To be made perfect is to be fulfilled.

Above all then, for the sake of all those who had died without seeing the promises they trusted in fulfilled, the readers must endure suffering now for the promises of God in Christ Jesus. In him is the fulfillment of all the promises of the ages.

DIMENSION THREE: WHAT DOES THE BIBLE MEAN TO ME?

1. We live in a society where instant gratification of personal desires seems to be the main motivation in people. Yet Hebrews urges Christians to persevere for the sake of future promises. How can you, as a Christian, cope with this situation? How can the church meet this secular challenge?

2. We have read of the biblical heroes and heroines of the faith. Who are some Christian heroes and heroines of the faith that we can use as role models? (These can be people of the past or people living now.)

Let us run with perseverance the race
marked out for us (12:1).

5

The Demands of Enduring Faith

Hebrews 12–13

DIMENSION ONE:
WHAT DOES THE BIBLE SAY?

Answer these questions by reading Hebrews 12

1. The readers of Hebrews are called to take three positive steps in 12:1-2. List them below.

2. The writer of Hebrews viewed the struggles of the Christian as the discipline of God. How should the discipline of God be understood by the Christian? (12:5-7)

3. For what two things ought we to strive as we run our race of life? (12:14)

4. Trouble that defiles many is the opposite of peace with all (12:14-15). What is the best guard against this cause of trouble? (12:15)

5. Why were the Israelites and even Moses fearful at the place where they met God? (12:18-21)

6. Thanks to the new covenant that Jesus mediated, what will be the nature of the heavenly assembly of God's people? (12:22-24)

7. Why will the earth and the heaven be shaken once more? (12:25-27)

8. As a part of an unshakable kingdom, what two things are Christians urged to do? (12:28)

Answer these questions by reading Hebrews 13

9. How many admonitions are given to the readers of Hebrews in 13:1-5?

10. List the three things Christians should do in respect to their leaders. (13:7)

11. Where did the sacrificial suffering of Jesus take place? (13:12)

12. Identify three sacrifices Christians are to offer to God. (13:15-16)

13. The writer asked his readers specifically to pray for what? (13:18-19)

14. The writer included a prayer for his readers. What did he ask of God for them? (13:20-21)

DIMENSION TWO: WHAT DOES THE BIBLE MEAN?

We are the climax of the call to faith and endurance in Hebrews. The writer has laid the foundation for his great exhortation in Chapters 1 through 10:18. He has emphasized the superiority of Jesus, God's Son, as the revealer of the will of God and as the redeemer of God's people. Jesus is presented as both the ultimate sacrifice for sin and the presiding high priest. Jesus also is seen as mediating a new covenant with better promises.

From Abel through Abraham, Moses, the judges, and the prophets, the writer has told the stories of a stream of faithful heroes and heroines. He says these persons struggled, conquered, and suffered for the sake of the unrealized promises of God (10:19–11:40). But now, in the very time of his readers, the writer reveals that the fulfillment of those promises is being realized in Jesus Christ. He challenges his readers to receive those promises by rejecting apostasy and enduring in faith. Finally, the writer warns and encourages the readers and details the demands of enduring faith.

❑ *Hebrews 12:1-2. Therefore* signals not only a look back but also a look ahead. All those faithful heroes and heroines of the past that were listed in Chapter 11 are here pictured as gazing down on the arena of life as if from a heavenly balcony. Their being "made perfect" (11:40) depends on the success of the faithful in the arena. The readers of Hebrews are the runners in the race.

With the encouragement of these witnesses, the writer urges the readers (and includes himself) to put off the weight of sin. Sin can hamper the performance of the Christian. Putting off sin for the Christian in the race of life is like the athlete who puts off the weights used in training. Sin is the tendency toward slackness, weakness, and apostasy. The race is long, demanding perseverance rather than speed.

Encouraged by the crowd of witnesses, the readers are urged to look to Jesus. He is an example of perseverance, and he is the one who has reached the goal. He is waiting there for those who persevere in the race to arrive. Jesus broke the trail for us, making it easier for us to follow him. He is the source and the end of the believer's faith. As Jesus persevered to the end, so he came to know the joy of attainment. He is seated at the right hand of the throne of God. Jesus persevered and won. The point is clear to the readers who are running the race. You, too, can persevere and win.

❑ *Hebrews 12:3-11.* Jesus is an example not only of perseverance but also of one who endured suffering. The readers are to take his example as a source of inspiration when they are tempted to give up. This temptation is liable to hit them when they must endure the hostility of sinners, as Jesus did. He shed his blood in the process. The readers have not yet followed his example that far (12:4).

Verse 5 contains a question raised simply to stimulate the readers to think about the reason for trials, struggles, and tribulation. The readers are reminded through this passage that suffering is the method God uses for disciplining God's children. God punishes the sin and rewards suffering for the right. To suffer is to know God's love. Suffering is a sign of God's acceptance of the sufferer (12:6-7).

The discipline a child receives from a parent seems unpleasant at the time, but parents discipline their children, not the children of others. Such parental concern is a sign of belonging to the family. Discipline may be for the benefit of the parent for the short time we are children. God's discipline has no self-interest. God disciplines us throughout our life, rather than just for the short period of childhood, so we may come to partake of God's character.

God is holy, and in due time, what seems painful will result in people who are holy and righteous, if they submit to the discipline. This discipline brings "a harvest of righteousness and peace" (12:11).

❑ *Hebrews 12:12-17.* Our writer reminds his readers of the cloud of witnesses and of the example of Jesus as incentives for persevering in the race of life. He also indicates God's love and interest in believers, evident because they are undergoing the discipline of suffering. Now he exhorts them to persevere. Along with the exhortation he gives specific instructions that they are to follow if they are to persevere.

They are to "strengthen your feeble arms and weak knees" (12:12). The call is to shake off weakness and weariness. The limbs grow tired in a race. The readers are also to "make level paths" for their feet (12:13). The picture is of the group engaged in the race toward the heavenly goal. Included in the group are those weaker than others. The stronger persons can help smooth the way and encourage the weaker persons. While physical expressions are used here, they stand for spiritual weaknesses. The writer is calling for spiritual strength and endurance.

Besides the personal spiritual revival called for in 12:12-13, the readers are urged to actively pursue peace with other people and holiness before God. To "see the Lord" is to attain heaven, where God is seated.

Grace is God's favor (12:15). The example of Esau makes it clear that God's grace is a blessing to be inherited. The blessing is receiving the promises of God in Christ Jesus.

Obtaining the end result of God's favor is not guaranteed. Any runner in the group can become a source of contention. Such a person is one who lacks faith and shrinks back (Hebrews 10:38-39). Such a troubler can infect and affect many. Having drooping hands and weak knees is a danger sign that one might fall away and not obtain the grace of God.

Besides the problem of becoming apostate and being a "bitter root," a person may fall into the pattern of Esau. Esau is a good example of a person who chooses the fleeting pleasures of the moment and loses the lasting blessing. He is also an example of one who has no opportunity to change things back. Perseverance in the race is absolutely necessary for those who would reach the goal.

❏ *Hebrews 12:18-24.* Hebrews 12:18-21 describes the terrifying phenomena that confronted the Israelites when they came to Mount Sinai. There, in the presence of the awesome God, they agreed to keep the law. Even Moses, who was to ascend the mountain as the representative of the people, was filled with fear (Hebrews 12:21; Deuteronomy 19:12-13). So dangerous was the presence of God that even a beast who touched the mountain was under the sentence of death (Hebrews 12:20; Exodus 19:12-13). Under these circumstances, the human tendency is to draw back.

We have every reason, however, to draw near and to persevere under the new covenant (12:22-24). To be in the presence of God in the heavenly Jerusalem is to join a gathering of angels that is festive, not terrifying. Joined with the angels are those counted as "firstborn." They are enrolled in heaven; that is their place. Heaven is their home because they are under the new covenant. They have come to God without fear because the covenant was instituted by the blood of Jesus. He is the means by which they can stand before God without fear. They, with Jesus (the original firstborn), make up the assembly of the first-born.

❏ *Hebrews 12:25-29.* In light of the direct access to heaven through the new arrangement, three responses are called for:

1. do not refuse the One who is speaking from heaven (12:25);

2. be grateful for receiving a Kingdom that cannot be moved (12:28);

3. in appreciation, offer God acceptable worship (12:28). Even as Christians are to draw near confidently (4:16), reverence for God includes recognition of God's awesome power and holiness and gratitude for God's grace.

❏ *Hebrews 13:1-6.* The underlying thought that ties these six verses together is love. "Loving each other as brothers" is genuine concern for fellow Christians. Showing hospitality to strangers is an act of love. The strangers here are Christians passing through. Showing concern for those in prison and those being abused by non-Christians is important, the readers are told. (This verse echoes 10:32-34.) Showing genuine concern for our partner in marriage is important. Immorality and adultery are dishonorable and dishonoring to the innocent partner and to God. Be free from a concern (love) for money. To love God is to trust in God's provision for you. One who trusts in money cannot trust also in God. Christian contentment is based on confidence in God's love and concern for every one of God's children.

❏ *Hebrews 13:7-17.* The leaders here may have given their lives for their faith, since the reference is to "the outcome of their way of life." The basic content of their faith is the confession contained in 13:8. Imitating the leaders' faith will enable a person not to be "carried away by all kinds of strange teachings." Apparently the unorthodox teachings had to do with regulations about food. One's faith can best be nourished by considering God's grace (favor) to the believer.

The separation between those who serve the earthly tent (tabernacle) and those who follow Jesus is the subject of 13:10-16. The allusions are cloudy to us, but they were clear to the first readers of Hebrews. The essential ideas are as follows:

1. The blood of sacrifice sanctifies (makes the worshipers holy), but the body of a sacrificed animal was burned outside the camp (Tabernacle enclosure or Temple area).

2. The blood of Jesus was shed on the cross outside the Temple area and outside the city (outside the gate).

3. The earthly Jerusalem and Temple are not where the Christian is headed. "The city that is to come" is the heavenly Jerusalem, the goal of the Christian.

4. Therefore, bear the abuse Jesus bore outside the city. Join him and do not be led away by other teachings.

5. The Temple sacrifices are not those the Christian offers. Believers are called to offer up the sacrifice of praise to God through Jesus. God is pleased not only with the fruit of the lips of believers but also with the sacrifices of sharing with and doing good to others.

We can assume that praising God, doing good, and sharing are a part of the lives of the leaders the readers are called to imitate. Not only are these leaders to be imitated, they are to be obeyed. Their spiritual authority is to be accepted. The leaders have a heavy responsibility for which they will be held accountable. The readers are told, for your own good, accept the leadership in the right spirit, ungrudgingly.

❑ *Hebrews 13:18-19.* The *us* for which prayer is requested may refer to the leaders, including the writer. More likely, however, this is simply an editorial *us.* The prayer requested is that he may be restored to the readers soon. Apparently the writer was away from the community of Christians to whom he wrote. The reason for this absence may have been that he was in prison for his faith. That would explain why he stressed that he had a clear conscience and always desired to act honorably.

❑ *Hebrews 13:20-21.* A measure of the sensitive spirit of the writer toward the readers is this prayer. He does not only ask them to pray for him; he underlines the importance of mutual prayer by praying for them.

In its simplest form the prayer is that God will equip the readers to do God's will, enabling them to do what is pleasing in God's sight. God is not addressed directly, however. The indirect address to God is in line with the manner in which a commoner might address a king. Peace is well-being and is related to having all one's debts paid up. Jesus, the Prince of Peace, has reconciled God and humankind, having paid the debt of sin. This act was in the plan of God, who raised Jesus from the dead. Jesus is the master leader, the great shepherd of the flock of God.

❏ *Hebrews 13:22-25.* Before sending his appeal off to the first readers, the writer added a postscript. First, he asked them to bear with the exhortations he had sent. His presentation was likely to irritate some of the readers.

The reference to "our brother Timothy" supports the view that the writer may have been in prison when he wrote Hebrews. Timothy was quite young when he began traveling with Paul. He likely outlived the apostle and would have been well-known after the first apostles died. The writer anticipated that he would see the readers in the company of Timothy.

Greetings are extended to leaders and to "all God's people," the members of the Christian community.

We do not know where Hebrews was written, but the reference to "those from Italy" suggests that it was not written in Italy.

DIMENSION THREE:
WHAT DOES THE BIBLE MEAN TO ME?

1. What are your motivations for running the race of life? (Read Hebrews 12:1-2 again to stimulate your thought.) What motivations for living the Christian life does your church encourage?

2. Hebrews 13:1-6 encourages the readers to practice love in their lives. In what ways are you implementing this exhortation in your life now? How can you increase your level of involvement in genuine caring? To what degree is your church committed to genuine concern for others?

3. The writer of Hebrews both requested prayer on his behalf and prayed on behalf of other believers. How important is intercessory prayer to your life, both as one who prays for others and as one for whom others pray? How does your church encourage such prayer among its members?

If any of you lacks wisdom, . . . ask God,
who gives generously to all without
finding fault, and it will be given to him (1:5).

—— 6 ——

A Manual of Wise
Instruction, Part 1
James 1–2

DIMENSION ONE:
WHAT DOES THE BIBLE SAY?

Answer these questions by reading James 1

1. What should happen when a Christian meets various trials? (1:2-3)

2. Under what conditions will God answer a request for wisdom? (1:5-8)

3. How does temptation develop into death? (1:14-15)

4. What happens to the person who looks into the perfect law that gives freedom and perseveres? (1:25)

5. James provided a concise definition of pure religion. What is it? (1:27)

Answer these questions by reading James 2

6. Why should a Christian show as much respect to a poor person as to a rich person? (2:5)

7. What is the royal law believers are expected to fulfill? (2:8)

8. What example of dead faith does James give? (2:14-17)

9. What two Old Testament examples does James use to prove that faith is completed by deeds? (2:21-25)

DIMENSION TWO:
WHAT DOES THE BIBLE MEAN?

You will recall that Hebrews is more like a lengthy, written sermon than a letter. It has no opening salutation or paragraph of thanksgiving. Paul's letters normally have a doctrinal section in the first half of each letter followed by ethical exhortations in the last half. Hebrews contains a number of exhortations scattered throughout the letter.

James, like Hebrews, is not a letter in the usual sense. James does have a short salutation. Following the salutation is a series of observations and instructions. These are loosely strung together, sometimes with no apparent direct relationship of topics.

James also has some similarities to the Book of Proverbs. Proverbs also is a collection of wise sayings and instructions intended to help a person acquire wisdom and live life wisely. James appears to be a collection of wise observations that will help a person live a Christian life in the midst of trials and temptations.

❏ *The Writer.* The name *James* is the first word in this book. A New Testament writer usually identified himself at the beginning, so we can assume that James is the writer. He also calls himself "a servant of God and of the Lord Jesus Christ" (1:1). In 3:1, the writer identifies himself as a teacher. The problem is to determine which James was the writer.

Two apostles were named James—James the son of Zebedee and James the son of Alphaeus (Matthew 10:2-3). The first James was executed around A.D. 44 (Acts 12:2), before the probable date when the letter was written. Most scholars have also rejected the idea that James the son of Alphaeus is the writer.

The most likely James to be the writer of this letter is the brother of Jesus (Galatians 1:19). The family of Jesus at first rejected him as the Messiah/Christ, except for Mary, his mother. Near the end of Jesus' ministry, however, they seem to have realized who he was. The brothers of Jesus, along with Mary, were in the upper room after the ascension of Jesus and just before the coming of the Holy Spirit on the day of Pentecost (Acts 1:12-14).

James is mentioned several times in the New Testament as a leader in the Jerusalem church (Acts 12:17; 15:13; 21:18; Galatians 2:9). He was the most influential leader there from about A.D. 40 until his death in A.D. 62. James was admired even by non-Christians for his pious life. He came to be known as James the Just. Tradition says James met a martyr's death, probably stoned to death at the instigation of the high priest.

Whether James the Just, the brother of Jesus, wrote the letter has been argued, even shortly after the period of the apostles. But Origen (A.D. 185–254) considered James the Just writer of the book. Jerome (A.D. 340–420) included James in his translation of the Old and New Testaments into Latin (the Vulgate). Official approval came at the Council of Carthage in A.D. 397.

For the purposes of our study, we will assume that the writer is James, the brother of Jesus. The problem of authorship has no direct bearing on the validity of the Book of James as authoritative Scripture. Generations of Christians from early in the history of the church have turned to James for instruction in Christian living. We, too, can find instruction and inspiration in James for individuals and for the church in the midst of the trials and temptations of our day.

❏ *Place of Writing.* If James the Just wrote the Letter of James, then he wrote in Jerusalem. All evidence indicates that James was a resident of Jerusalem within a few years after Jesus' death and lived there during the last decades of his life.

❏ *The Readers.* In the salutation (1:1), the writer addresses "the twelve tribes scattered among the nations." This expression refers to the Christians scattered all over the Roman Empire. The letter could have been addressed to Jewish Christians only, or, more likely, to mixed groups of Jewish and Gentile Christians.

❏ *Purpose of the Letter.* This manual of wise instruction is intended to strengthen the faith of the readers in the midst of the difficulties of life. James gives counsel on subjects about which every Christian ought to be on guard.

❏ *James 1:1.* *James* is the Greek form of the Hebrew name *Jacob.* As with Saul who became Paul, many Hebrews had Greek and Hebrew forms of their names.

James considered himself "a *servant* [a slave], of God and of the Lord Jesus Christ." Paul used this term about himself (Romans 1:1; Philippians 1:1; Titus 1:1). Christians are "bought at a price" and are not their own (1 Corinthians 6:20). They belong to Christ.

❏ *James 1:2-4.* When faith is tested, it is either crushed because it is too weak or it is made stronger. The stronger the faith, the more steadfast the Christian. A really mature faith (perfect and complete) can result from many trials.

Since steadfastness comes through testing, James tells his readers to consider various trials sources of joy. Nothing should make a believer happier than to know nothing is lacking in his or her relationship to Jesus Christ.

❏ *James 1:5-8.* Christians need wisdom to help them meet temptations. When James writes, "If any of you lacks wisdom," he assumes that some of them do lack wisdom. "The fear of the Lord is the beginning of knowledge; / but fools despise wisdom and discipline" (Proverbs 1:7). Knowledge consists of facts learned; wisdom guides in the use of knowledge.

The main point of this section, however, is not wisdom but how to obtain wisdom. God is the source of wisdom. To obtain it, ask. Pray for it. Jesus said, "Ask and it will be given to you" (Matthew 7:7). But let the request for wisdom be a prayer of faith. Doubting while asking is the mark of a person unstable in the faith.

❏ *James 1:9-11.* The "brother in humble circumstances" (Christian) is poor, yet he has reason to boast (to glory in the high position God has accorded him, 2:5). Many poor people were members of the early church (1 Corinthians 1:26).

The rich (Christian), on the other hand, has nothing to boast in except being humbled. Wealth can puff a person up with pride, yet a Christian is called to be humble (4:6). Riches mean nothing in the moment of death. The person who lives only to acquire wealth will die empty-handed in the midst of that pursuit. Christians must hold a balanced view of poverty and wealth.

❏ *James 1:12-18.* Besides developing steadfastness, the person who endures receives the victory crown. The "crown of life" should make any Christian happy.

This instruction makes clear that God is not the source of temptation. God is the source of "every good and perfect gift" (1:17). The source of temptation is a person's own desire. Desire is neither good nor evil; desire is neutral. But desire lures and entices. Unchecked, the effect can be deadly. Desire produces sin, and sin can develop into a complete separation from God. That separation is death in the most profound sense.

Desire can be controlled. With every temptation God will provide a way of escape (1 Corinthians 10:13).

As first fruits, we are to offer ourselves to God as a living sacrifice (Romans 12:1). The first fruits are always God's.

❏ *James 1:19-27.* What James wants the "dear brothers" to know is given in these verses. He gives wise advice indeed. Everyone should listen carefully and think before speaking. The quick answer often comes off the top of one's head and out of anger. The warning is to be "slow to become angry." Anger is ranked here with moral filth and evil (1:21).

Uncontrolled anger is unacceptable behavior for a Christian. It accomplishes no good for God. In fact, an angry Christian can be a stumbling block to those outside of Christ.

Hearing the word is not enough; to hear and not to do is to fool ourselves. The illustration of forgetfulness in 1:23-25 is quite clear. The sincere believer who looks into the mirror of God's Word cannot forget that in Christ there is freedom from sin and the liberty to love (Galatians 5:13) Looking intently into the perfect law moves the person of faith to action. That person is blessed in the process.

Religion, as James defines it, requires deeds, not empty words without appropriate actions. Pure and faultless religion requires no words. It requires visiting the weak and vulnerable in society so as to supply their needs. To keep oneself from being polluted by the world is to guard against adopting the selfish view of the world, else giving to the needy will cease.

❏ *James 2:1-13.* We are always in danger of showing favoritism in the church. This problem must have existed in the early church also, or this teaching would not have been included. An example of what was going on is given in 2:2-4.

Favoritism is not acceptable to those who trust in the saving grace of Jesus (2:9). The ground is level at the foot of the cross. All are saved by grace through faith, as a gift of God, and none are worthy. Snobbish distinctions among believers are unwarranted.

The rich tend to love riches. Jesus taught that we cannot love God and money (Matthew 6:24). The rich trust in wealth; the poor cannot. They trust in God.

Further, the love of money is the root of all kinds of evil (1 Timothy 6:10), including the evil of oppressing the poor (James 2:6). The rich shall insult the poor and deal unjustly with them, dragging them into court. In the process they speak badly against the poor Christian and so against the name of Christ.

The rich persons James has in mind in this context apparently are not rich Christians, as perhaps in 1:10-11. They are wealthy non-Christians from the community who have come to visit the assembly, either on someone's invitation or out of curiosity.

The correct Christian practice is to love others without showing favoritism. That is the royal law of love that Jesus taught (Matthew 22:39).

In 2:12-13, James concludes his teaching on snobbery. Christians should speak and act with the Last Judgment in mind. God has graciously covered our sins by the blood of Jesus Christ, but we can hardly expect to be shown mercy for the sin of favoritism if we practice it. We are to be hearers *and* doers of the word.

❑ *James 2:14-26.* James opens this section with a question. The answer he expects his readers to give is "Nothing." In 2:17, he answers his own question by stating that faith without deeds is dead. Such faith is profitless; it will not save. The case study he presents shows a person saying sympathetic words. These are the words expected of a person of faith. But the work of faith, the vital deed, is left undone.

Verse 18 is a statement that responds to what James has presented in 2:14-17. "Someone" distinguishes between faith and deeds. James responds immediately. Faith and deeds are two sides to the same coins. They cannot be separated. To prove his point, James provides three examples. The first example is of belief without deeds (demons). Two biblical examples follow.

Abraham was justified by deeds when he was willing to offer Isaac on the altar (Genesis 22). In Romans 4:1-12, the apostle Paul uses Abraham as an example. But he declares that Abraham was justified by faith apart from deeds. Do Paul and James contradict each other on the matter of faith and deeds? No. Paul is talking about deeds *in order to be saved* (they are of no value). James is talking about deeds *as a result of being saved* (they prove faith).

Rahab (Joshua 2:1-21) is another example of this basic principle. She saved the lives of the explorers Joshua sent to Jericho. Rahab acted on her faith that God had given the land into the hands of the Israelites (Joshua 2:9). Her name is on the list of the heroic faithful in Hebrews (11:31).

James draws this conclusion: A human body without the spirit is dead. It cannot fulfill a purpose or function. Just so, faith without deeds is without value. It is profitless.

DIMENSION THREE:
WHAT DOES THE BIBLE MEAN TO ME?

1. How can I guard myself from permitting desire to produce sin in my life (James 1:13-15)? How can the church play a supporting role in such efforts?

2. How can I be confident that I have a pure and faultless religion before God (James 1:27)?

*The wisdom that comes from heaven is first of all
pure; then peaceloving, considerate, submissive,
full of mercy and good fruit, impartial and sincere (3:17).*

7

A Manual of Wise Instruction, Part 2

James 3–5

DIMENSION ONE: WHAT DOES THE BIBLE SAY?

Answer these questions by reading James 3

1. Why does James discourage many of his readers from becoming teachers? (3:1)

2. What evidence does James provide to show that the tongue is "a restless evil, full of deadly poison"? (3:7-10)

3. How does James describe the wisdom that does not come from heaven? (3:15-16)

4. What are the characteristics of the wisdom that comes from heaven? (3:17)

Answer these questions by reading James 4

5. Why do people fight, quarrel, and kill? (4:1-2)

6. What positive actions can believers take to show humility and receive God's grace? (4:6-8)

7. Who is capable of judging another Christian? (4:12)

8. To what statement does James refer when he says, "You boast and brag"? (4:13-16a)

Answer these questions by reading James 5

9. James foretold that the rich would suffer miseries (5:1-6). Why would this come upon them in the last days?

10. James gives three examples of patient people in 5:7-11. Identify them.

11. Why is James against swearing by an oath? (5:12)

12. What are James's recommendations for people who are (1) in trouble, (2) happy, or (3) sick? (5:13-14)

13. Who is a good example of a righteous man whose prayers were effective? (5:16b-18)

14. What is the proper thing to do when a Christian brother or sister wanders from the truth? (5:19-20)

DIMENSION TWO:
WHAT DOES THE BIBLE MEAN?

This lesson continues the study of James's wise instruction that we began in Lesson 6. The subjects covered in this lesson are (1) the tongue is dangerous—bridle it, (2) instruction on the wise way to live, (3) observations on the arrogant and the dishonest wealthy, and (4) wise comments on various subjects.

❑ *James 3:1-12.* The subject of bridling the tongue was introduced in 1:19-27. But there the focus is on being quick to hear, slow to speak, slow to anger. Here, the attention of the reader is drawn to the importance of controlling the tongue.

This section is made up of three segments. James 3:1-2a (through "We all stumble in many ways") introduces the problem of proper speech. Then 3:2-5a (through "but it makes great boasts") is a paragraph on the difficulty of controlling the tongue, and 3:5b-12 is a second supporting paragraph on the danger of a poisonous tongue. We will examine these segments in order.

The wisdom and ability to teach was recognized as an important spiritual gift God gives for the upbuilding of the church (1 Corinthians 12:28; Ephesians 4:11). Those who possess and exercise the gift follow a high calling. Jesus is an example to follow; he was a superb teacher.

Many of the believers who were to read this letter must have thought themselves called to be teachers. James warns against taking on the responsibility of teaching too lightly. Teaching is a calling that is privileged, but the teacher is liable to more severe condemnation for errors than the lay person. James is aware of the weight of the teaching responsibility. This letter is proof of his conscientious work as a teacher.

Teachers, like everyone else, make mistakes (3:2a). But teachers bear a greater burden of liability for mistakes. Teachers' errors may affect the salvation of those who hear. So what teachers do with the tongue is loaded with important consequences.

The point of 3:2b-5a is that something large can be controlled by controlling a vital, smaller part of it. A controlled tongue is vital to the control of the entire self. Perhaps James had in mind that teachers should be careful about what they say and how they say it. But the general rule applies to everyone. The mature (perfect) person (3:2b) so carefully controls the tongue as to make no speaking blunders.

What the tongue says is directly linked to what the mind thinks, as Jesus indicated (Mark 7:21-22). Out of the abundance of the heart the mouth speaks (Luke 6:45). The Christian is to be transformed by the renewing of the mind (Romans 12:2). While this is an ongoing process, the result will include controlling the tongue so that evil speech, slander, and foolishness do not gush forth.

James 3:5b-6 uses the metaphor of a raging fire to describe how dangerous the tongue can be. We know how destructive brush and forest fires are. Imagine how much greater the danger was in ancient times, before the development of modern firefighting equipment and techniques.

A forest fire is awesome in its devastating power. It can destroy the one who set it, whether accidentally or on purpose, and it can destroy them. A tongue that strikes sparks sets off consuming fires of anger, revenge, and retaliation. The tongue used maliciously can be a devastating instrument of destruction.

The tongue is a fire kindled from hellfire. That is, Satan is the source of acid, burning speech.

James 3:6b-12 makes clear that James has evil speech in mind. The tongue is depicted as "a world of evil" with vast potential for unrighteousness. The tongue is a restless evil, constantly wiggling like a snake on the go and venomous as a rattler.

The background of 3:7 is Genesis 1:28; 2:19; and 9:2. Humans are given the power to rule over animals. But who can tame the tongue? No one alone, but by God's grace it is possible.

In James 3:9-12, the tongue is recognized as the instrument of deception. We expect consistency in nature. We expect a good spring to produce good drinking water. We expect a brackish spring to flow with undrinkable water. We expect fruit trees and vines to produce after their kind. We expect the ocean water to be salty, not fresh. So, we should be able to expect consistency in the speech that comes forth from the mouth of a Christian. But the evil, uncontrolled tongue spews forth from the same source both blessings and curses.

Christians should be slow to speak. They should refrain from speaking in anger. "Do not let any unwholesome talk come out of your mouths, but only what is helpful for building others up, . . . that it may benefit those who listen" (Ephesians 4:29).

❏ *James 3:13–4:12.* There seems to be no direct connection between this section and the one preceding. James 3:13–4:12 is mainly concerned with how to live a good life. James emphasizes three aspects.

❏ *James 3:13-18.* James opens this section with a question. The answer follows immediately. The good life he has in mind in 3:13 includes the characteristics listed in 3:17-18. The "humility that comes from wisdom" is the opposite of bitter envy and selfish ambition (3:14).

Humbleness is not weakness. Humbleness is strength controlled by gentleness. Jesus was humble but not weak. One of the Beatitudes speaks of the meek (Matthew 5:5).

Paul exhorted Christian teachers not to be quarrelsome but to be kindly toward everyone, to be forbearing, and to correct those in need of correction with gentleness (2 Timothy 2:24-

25a). Peter urged defenders of the faith to speak gently and reverently (1 Peter 3:15b).

James compares and contrasts earthly wisdom with the wisdom that is "from heaven"—heavenly wisdom. Earthly wisdom looks at circumstances in an unspiritual, even a demonic way (3:15). Selfish ambition, boasting, bitter jealousy, and lying are evidences of worldly wisdom. This world view does not bring the good life or peace. It results in disorder, conflict, and the most inhumane actions that one person can do to another.

Contrast the wisdom "from heaven" with the wisdom of the world. The wisdom from heaven is pure. A Christian is cleansed by the blood of Jesus Christ and that person's mind is set on things that are above (Colossians 3:2). The peace of God that passes all understanding is available to the believer (Philippians 4:7) because of the reconciliation with God and other persons. Christians are to be open to reason, full of mercy because they know what it means to have received mercy from God, and full of good fruits.

❏ *James 4:1-10.* The preceding section ends with reference to *peace.* James now turns his attention to the opposite—war.

We saw earlier that desire can lead to sin and death (1:14-15). Here a person's desires are recognized as the cause of quarrels and fightings.

In 4:2-3, James leaves no doubt about the cause of quarrels. Desire can even lead to murder. Coveting not only breaks the tenth commandment (Exodus 20:17), it also leads to savage efforts to obtain what is coveted.

The Christian has but to ask in order to receive all that is *needed* (Matthew 7:7-8). But God does not promise all that is *desired.* Needs are not measured by desires.

The expression *adulterous people* in James 4:4 actually says "Adulterers and Adulteresses" in the original language. Many times in the Bible spiritual infidelity is spoken of as adultery (Hosea 3:1, for example). Jesus used a similar expression: "this adulterous and sinful generation" (Mark 8:38).

The wisdom "from heaven" may be received by Christians simply by asking for it (James 1:5). They then commit spiritual adultery if they live by the wisdom of this world, if they are driven by their desires (4:4).

The exact quotation in 4:5 cannot be found in the Bible, nor has it been found in other known writings. The general thought occurs in Genesis 6:5-6a and Isaiah 63:8-16. The spirit God has made to live in us may be the human spirit, created in God's image. Or, the spirit may refer to the indwelling Holy Spirit given as a gift to those who come to God through Christ.

The quotation in 4:6 is from Proverbs 3:34. This proverb supports the view that God gives abundant grace to the humble.

The wise way to live requires two actions (4:7-10); (1) submission to God as evidence of humility and (2) resistance to the devil to provide the way of escape from the temptations that desire and passion arouse.

Repentance, shown by sincere sorrow (4:9), is essential to receiving the gift of the Holy Spirit (salvation) through God's grace (Acts 2:38). Repentance, a complete reversal of the way one thinks and acts, is evidence of true humility.

Humility is an essential ingredient in the make-up of a sincere follower of Christ. Christ provides the perfect example of humility for his followers: "And being found in appearance as a man, he humbled himself and became obedient to death—even death on a cross" (Philippians 2:8). Humility is the opposite of the pride and vanity that characterize the wisdom of the world.

❏ *James 4:11-12.* James 4:11 contains a direct prohibition against one Christian condemning another. Of course, all are sinners saved by grace. Judgmental thinking about other believers followed by "slander" (harsh, critical words) judges rather than obeys the law. That is, a judgmental person has, in practice, rejected the royal law to love neighbor as self (2:8). Further, the judgmental Christian assumes the authority of God. The Creator alone is able to save and to destroy (Matthew 10:28).

❏ *James 4:13–5:6.* This section teaches against boasting and bragging (4:13-17) and against ill-gotten gain (5:1-6).

The objection in 4:13-17 is not against good business planning. What James objects to is the arrogance of Christians who plan ventures without any thought of the One who controls history.

Such planners lack humility and a sense of living under the lordship of Christ. Their thinking and actions reflect a bad (inappropriate) way for Christians to think. They reflect the wisdom that is not from above. Even worse is the person who knows what to do and fails to do it. That error is grievous; it is missing the mark of God's will, and that is sin.

James apparently addresses his remarks in 5:1-6 to the rich outside the church. Echoes of what he says may also apply to wealthy Christians.

The rich are often considered happy and carefree, in contrast to the poor who are burdened with labor in order to obtain the necessities of life. But the poor are a special concern of God (5:4). The "ears of the Lord Almighty" heard the cries of the Israelites under their Egyptian oppressors too.

James calls on the rich to weep and wail in anticipation of the coming "last days" and the judgment of God (5:3). All the treasure they have laid up will prove to be worthless. In fact, what they have laid up will be evidence of their greed. What they trusted in will then destroy them, consuming them like fire.

❏ *James 5:7-11.* Encouragement to patience is needed in the face of economic oppression. Patience is also useful in other circumstances of life. The patience of the farmer is a good example. The farmer plants and must wait throughout the growing season for the harvest (5:7). The readers are urged to be as patient for the coming of Jesus Christ as the farmer is for the harvest (5:8).

Rather than grumbling and impatience (5:9-10), believers are called to suffering and patience. Two examples of suffering and patience are given to encourage the readers. The prophets suffered for speaking "in the name of the Lord." Job remained steadfast despite the afflictions imposed on him at the hand of Satan. In the end Job was blessed with the compassion and mercy of God.

❏ *James 5:12.* What James says here echoes the words of Jesus in Matthew 5:34-37. What James condemned was confirming the most mundane matters by an oath. Christians should always speak the truth; for the Christian, *yes* should mean "yes" and *no* should mean "no" without further emphasis.

❑ *James 5:13-18.* Christians can do some things for themselves. If they are suffering, they can pray. The redeemed of God have much to be grateful for, even in the midst of suffering and trouble. Let the cheerful sing praises.

James provides a prescription for the sick. Call for the elders of the church to pray over and anoint that person with oil "in the name of the Lord."

Sometimes sin is the cause of sickness. Confession can be therapeutic. We all need to confess our errors to one another and to pray for one another. Prayer is the key to healing, following confession. Elijah is a good example of the truth expressed in 5:16b. (See his story in 1 Kings 17–18.)

❑ *James 5:19-20.* In closing James shows his shepherd's heart. One can wander (backslide) away from the caring, sharing fellowship of the church depicted in 5:13-18. To do so is to wander from the truth of the gospel, the basis of the church. Wanderers are worthy of being brought back.

Those who bring wanderers back know that a sinner (the wanderer) has been saved from eternal death (Revelation 21:8).

DIMENSION THREE:
WHAT DOES THE BIBLE MEAN TO ME?

1. Which of these concerns are problems in your Christian experience: Controlling the tongue (3:1-12)? Acting on the wisdom not from above rather than the wisdom from above (3:13-18)? Controlling your passions and desires (4:1-10)? Being judgmental (4:11-12)? Planning without thought for the Lord (4:13-17)? Which are problems you see in your church?

2. How can you increase your effectiveness as a positive influence in the life of your church (5:13-18)?

Live such good lives among the pagans that
. . . they may see your good deeds and glorify God (2:12).

— 8 —
How to Live in
a Hostile World
1 Peter

DIMENSION ONE:
WHAT DOES THE BIBLE SAY?

Answer these questions by reading 1 Peter

1. To whom is this letter addressed? (1:1)

2. What was the basis of the living hope in which the readers rejoiced? (1:3b)

3. What did the prophets predict about Christ? (1:10-11)

4. If someone claims God as Father, what effect should the claim have on that person's manner of life? (1:14-16)

5. What four expressions are used to describe all those who have received mercy? (2:9-10)

6. If we follow in the steps of Jesus, what specific things will we try to do? (2:21-23)

7. In relation to one another, how should wives and husbands act? (3:1, 7)

8. What characteristics should Christians show toward one another? (3:8)

9. First Peter 4:7-11 lists a number of practices Christians should follow. Why should Christians practice these things? (4:11b)

10. Suffering as a Christian is acceptable, but Christians are warned not to suffer for certain things. What are they? (4:15)

11. Identify the main theme in 1 Peter 5:1-6.

12. First Peter 5:7-11 has two comforting promises for Christians. What are they?

DIMENSION TWO:
WHAT DOES THE BIBLE MEAN?

The First Letter of Peter is a message of instruction and encouragement for believers who are under the stress of trials and persecution. First Peter's content and tone of expression have strengthened Christians from the first through the twentieth centuries.

❏ *Writer, Date, and Place of Writing.* The first word in the opening verse of the letter indicates that the apostle Peter is the writer. This use of Peter's name has not settled the matter, however. Some experts have argued that Peter could not have been the author because

1. a simple Galilean fisherman would not have been capable of the high level of Greek the letter is written in;

2. the harsh persecution of the church in Asia Minor did not take place until several decades after Peter's death;

3. Peter would not likely have expressed his ideas in language as similar to Paul's as is found in the letter;

4. the close relationship Peter had with Jesus is not reflected in the letter.

Scholars who accept this evidence assume that the letter was written by a disciple of Peter in the apostle's name about A.D. 112.

Each of these points can be countered:

1. Peter dictated and Silas wrote the Greek (5:12);

2. persecution of the church was a reality in the time of Peter;

3. Peter and Paul drew from a common stock of expressions about the faith;

4. to say that the close bond between Peter and Jesus is not reflected in the letter is an overstatement.

We will assume that Peter had Silas write the letter and that he (Peter) approved it. The writing would have been done before Peter's death as a martyr in Rome around A.D. 64. The rejection of his authorship is based on thin circumstantial evidence. In addition, early witnesses in the church, such as Irenaeus, support the traditional view of Peter's authorship.

The belief that Rome was the place of origin for the letter is based on the view that "Babylon" (5:13) is really a reference to Rome. Similar usage is found in the Book of Revelation (14:8; 17:5; 18:2).

❏ *The Readers.* The letter is addressed to Christians living in five provinces of Asia Minor (part of modern Turkey). They lived in the region originally evangelized by Paul. The congregations likely consisted of Jewish and Gentile Christians. That situation is reflected in the stories of the missionary journeys of Paul and his companions to the region found in the Book of Acts.

❏ *1 Peter 1:1-2.* Peter's Hebrew name is Simon Bar (son of) Jonah (Matthew 16:17), the equivalent to Simon Johnson (son of John). Jesus gave him a nickname that stuck: *Cephas,* meaning "rock." The Greek equivalent is *Petros*—in English, *Peter.*

"Scattered throughout" was discussed in connection with "The Readers of James" (page 51). The readers are also described as "chosen according to the foreknowledge of God." God takes the initiative, and whosoever will respond may come. Those who respond are also consecrated by the Holy Spirit. They are chosen, destined, and sanctified to the end that they will obey Jesus Christ and be purified through his shed blood. Those two involved verses set the stage for everything that follows in the letter. The readers have been set apart to live holy lives in a hostile world.

❏ *1 Peter 1:3-12.* Peter, perhaps in his early sixties, still stands amazed at the grace of God in Christ Jesus. He has never lost the sense of wonder at what he witnessed and experienced. He must bless God. Peter wants the Christians to whom he writes to appreciate their new life in Christ as well. This new life

1. is the result of God's great mercy (1:3b);
2. provides a living hope (1:3b);

3. is based on the reality of the resurrection of Jesus from the dead, because that holds promise of the believer's resurrection (1:3b; 1 Corinthians 15:16-23).

4. gives a living hope that goes beyond resurrection to include a heavenly inheritance, described in the timeless adjectives of 1:4.

No wonder Peter blessed God.

Those "chosen according to the foreknowledge of God" can rest assured that their inheritance is kept in heaven for them. They can also be confident that through faith God's power will guard them so that they will receive their inheritance (1:4-5).

The tried and true faith of believers will bring praise, honor, and glory to Christ at his second coming and to them as they share in it (1:7). Even now their faith brings them joy beyond expression, and the fulfillment of faith is salvation.

Peter is not quite through with this poetic appreciation of salvation. His readers have received what prophets could only see and marvel at in visions (1:10-12). Servants of God that they were, it was revealed to them that what they dimly perceived would be seen completely in the period in which Peter was living. And more, the readers were participants in such a marvelous salvation that even the angels knew not the details before the fullness of time had come.

❑ *1 Peter 1:13–2:10.* Peter has pointed out to his readers the incredibly great blessings of being chosen, destined, and sanctified by God's grace. The new life requires an appropriate response. He calls on the readers to live a holy life before God.

❑ *1 Peter 1:13.* To "prepare" the mind is to establish a determined mindset. Middle Eastern men wore robes in biblical times. They would gird up the ends around the waist in preparation for strenuous activities. The same theme of serious determination continues in the rest of the verse. Quite literally, Christians were to "prepare . . . for action."

❑ *1 Peter 1:14–2:3.* While Peter uses the plural, *children,* what he calls for in Christian conduct must be done individually. Notice the major emphases:

1. obedience is called for (1:14);
2. be holy like the Holy One (1:15-16);

3. live out your time here on earth (in exile) with reverent respect for the Father to whom you pray (1:17);

4. have confidence in God because of Jesus (1:21);

5. love one another earnestly with all your heart (1:22);

6. "rid yourselves of" malice (wickedness), deceit (guile), hypocrisy (pretense), envy (jealousy), and all slander (insulting language) (2:1);

7. "crave" the pure spiritual milk, the word of God (2:1).

❑ *1 Peter 2:4-10.* To live as a Christian in a hostile world requires girding up the mind, purifying the soul, being born anew, putting away malice and the like, and craving spiritual food. But God's children do not exist in isolation. They are part of the family of God. The family metaphor used earlier now becomes a "spiritual house" metaphor (2:5).

The image of God's people as a house is related to the Temple in Jerusalem. The living Stone is Jesus Christ. The quotations in 2:6 (Isaiah 28:16), 2:7 (Psalm 118:22), and 2:8 (Isaiah 8:14) establish that fact.

Jesus also quoted Psalm 118:22 (Matthew 21:42). He saw himself as the stone rejected by the builders. But God made him the head of the corner.

Now the readers, who are also living stones, are instructed to be built into a spiritual house on the living foundation stone (2:5). They are also to be a holy priesthood in that living temple, presenting their bodies as living sacrifices to God (Romans 12:1).

Committed Christians belong to the family of God by the new birth. They have become a chosen race (Isaiah 43:20b), a royal priesthood, a holy nation (both from Exodus 19:6), God's own people (Exodus 19:5), like Israel of old. The purpose of God's people is given in 2:9. Verse 10 is based on Hosea 1:9-10.

❑ *1 Peter 2:11-12.* As God's people in exile, the readers are aliens in a Gentile world. They are to refrain from indulging selfish desires. These selfish desires war against the soul. God's people are to live a life that declares the wonderful deeds of God (1 Peter 2:9) through their own good deeds.

❑ *1 Peter 2:13-17.* As noncitizens, Christians are to submit to civil authorities for the sake of God's concern to redeem the lost and to guard God's people. Christians are to show appropriate respect (honor) to all.

❏ *1 Peter 2:18-20.* Slavery was a fact of life for many of Peter first readers. To live a holy life, a Christian slave must be submissive to the master. This submitting might require unjust suffering, but suffering can be endured if one is "conscious of God."

❏ *1 Peter 2:21-25.* Peter advised his readers to be patient in suffering and to follow in the footsteps of Jesus. God allowed Jesus to suffer on behalf of the believers, and they have benefited. Christian suffering for doing right will benefit others, also.

❏ *1 Peter 3:1-12.* Submission and consideration for others is a way of life for Christians.

❏ *1 Peter 3:1-7.* Wives are free in Christ to be submissive to their husbands. Husbands are to be considerate and understanding toward their wives. A wife is to be honored as one who is a joint heir of eternal life. Failure to treat one's wife considerately will affect one's spiritual life and communication with God.

❏ *1 Peter 3:8-12.* To live a holy life requires the Christian graces listed in 3:8. Peter then quotes from Psalm 34:12-16 to remind the readers that God favors right conduct.

❏ *1 Peter 3:13-22.* Within God's purpose and will, suffering for doing right may come. Jesus so suffered on our behalf (3:17-18).

One of the most difficult passages to understand that can be found in the New Testament appears in 3:19-20. Christ, through the spirit of inspiration in Noah, warned Noah's generation of the coming catastrophe. That generation is now "in prison," the place where the dead await judgment.

❏ *1 Peter 4:1-11.* The secret to suffering successfully is to think like Christ (Philippians 2:5-11). Like Christ, live by the will of God rather than by human passions.

The good news was preached to the dead while they were yet alive (4:6). God has had a witness in every generation (Romans 1:19-23).

Every generation of Christians has lived on the edge of the end of all things. The end of all things in this world comes for us the moment we die. Keep sane and sober, pray, love, be hospitable, use your spiritual gift or gifts now.

❏ *1 Peter 4:12-19.* Peter advises his beloved readers not to be surprised when fiery trials (persecutions) erupt. They are sojourners in an alien and hostile world.

Rather, be of good cheer when persecutions come; for by sharing in Christ's sufferings (the church is the body of Christ), you will also share in Christ's glory. Do not suffer as an evildoer.

❏ *1 Peter 5:1-11.* First Peter 5:1-4 is addressed to the leaders of the Christian community, "the elders." Peter shares the role of shepherding the flock of God, the people of the faith. He emphasizes gentle actions and a humble attitude. Humility now assures exaltation then, in God's tomorrow and by God's hand. Relax, Peter writes, God cares for you now.

First Peter 5:8-9 is just as valid as the preceding verses. The devil is the personification of evil, waiting to swallow up the unwary and enticing Christians to forgo the suffering, to cave in to their passions. Resist the devil!

You are not alone in resisting, Peter assures his readers. You are not alone in suffering. Suffering will end, and you will receive the reward for faithfulness—to share in the eternal glory of Christ.

❏ *1 Peter 5:12-14.* Silas was responsible for drafting the letter. He is probably the Silas of Acts 15:22-40.

The last part of 5:12 gives the specific reason why Peter wrote. The "true grace of God" is the readers' current situation of suffering. Find joy in it (4:13). "Stand fast in it."

Greetings from the church in Rome (Babylon) come with the letter. The Roman Christians, too, are chosen. Greetings also come from (John) Mark. We know Mark as the companion of Paul and Barnabas (Acts 15:37-40).

DIMENSION THREE:
WHAT DOES THE BIBLE MEAN TO ME?

What does being part of "a royal priesthood" mean to you? How can the priesthood of all believers be realized in your life and in the life of your church? (1 Peter 2:5, 9).

Be all the more eager to make your calling and election sure.
For if you do these things, you will never fall (1:10).

— 9 —
How to Handle the Crisis in the Church
2 Peter

DIMENSION ONE:
WHAT DOES THE BIBLE SAY?

Answer these questions by reading 2 Peter

1. How does Peter describe his relationship to Jesus Christ? (1:1)

2. What can the believers in the great and precious promises of God expect to receive? (1:4)

3. What one thing does Peter want to do for his readers? (1:12)

4. What were the sources of the apostolic witness and the prophetic word? (1:16-21)

5. What does Peter say that the false teachers will do? (2:1-3)

6. In 2:4-10a, Peter uses three examples to show that God knows how to keep the unrighteous under punishment. List the three examples.

7. The false teachers are seen as following in the footsteps of what biblical character? (2:12-16)

8. Why do the false teachers fail to deliver on their promise of freedom for their followers? (2:19)

9. Why do scoffers say, "Where is this 'coming' he promised?" (3:3-4)

10. Why does the Lord delay the day of judgment and destruction of ungodly people? (3:9)

11. According to the promise of God, for what do Christians wait? (3:13)

12. Peter warns the readers to beware of two related things. What are they? (3:15-17)

DIMENSION TWO:
WHAT DOES THE BIBLE MEAN?

Second Peter was written to remind the readers that their faith rested on the revelation of the prophets and the witness of the apostles. They must also be alert to the threat of false teachers who would deny the promise of the second coming of Christ and endanger the church. The faithful are urged to respond to the threat by holy living and growth in grace and knowledge of Jesus Christ.

❏ *Writer.* Who wrote Second Peter? That question has been debated by experts more than the authorship of any other book in the New Testament. As in First Peter, the letter opens with the name of the apostle. Either it was written by Peter, or it was written by someone else under his name.

Those who suspect that someone other than Peter wrote the letter do so because

1. in the earliest references to the letter in the period after the apostles (after A.D. 100), some doubt is expressed that Peter wrote the letter;

2. Eusebius, the fourth-century church historian, listed it among the disputed books;

3. this book differs from First Peter in the style of the Greek used;

4. Paul's writings are referred to as "Scripture" (3:16b), an expression reserved elsewhere in the New Testament for the Old Testament, therefore suggesting a date later than Peter's time.

5. Second Peter has strong resemblances to Jude, which many scholars date late in the first century.

Scholars following those lines of thought suspect that the letter was written by an unnamed follower of Peter.

On the side of Peter as the writer are these points:

1. the letter claims the authorship of Peter;

2. works from the same period written under assumed names normally contain heretical vies not found in this letter;

3. personal experiences of Peter, known from the Gospels, are referred to in the letter;

4. stylistic differences occur, but these are often noted without mentioning the many points of similarity with First Peter;

5. Paul claimed the inspiration of the Holy Spirit, so his letters could have been received as scripture when he wrote them;

6. similarities between Jude and Second Peter do not require borrowing as an explanation, nor dating in the same decade.

We cannot settle this controversy. For our purposes, however, we will view Peter as the writer of the letter.

❏ *Place and Date of Writing.* Peter speaks of his approaching death (1:14). According to early Christian tradition, Peter was martyred in Rome about the same time Paul was killed, between A.D. 64 and A.D. 67. Since Peter is aware that this time is near, we assume the letter was written in Rome.

❏ *The Readers.* Peter writes in 3:1 that this is the second letter to the readers. We can assume that it was written to the same audience as those mentioned in 1 Peter 1:1.

❏ *The Form of the Letter.* The letter lacks the normal closing of an epistle. It is similar in form to a "testament." Testaments are a literary type begun by Jews in the intertestamental period. A testament is a collection of the writer's important teachings written down on the occasion of the writer's impending death. Christians took up this literary form, and Second Peter is a good example.

❏ *2 Peter 1:1-2. Simeon* (1:1 in the NRSV) is another form of *Simon,* Peter's first name. Peter considers himself a servant as well as an apostle. Jesus said, "If anyone wants to be first, he must be the very last, and the servant of all" (Mark 9:35b).

Peter does not identify the place to which the letter was sent. In 3:1, he mentions a previous letter, however, so the recipients must be the same as in First Peter.

"Those who . . . have received a faith as precious as ours" likely are Gentile Christians. The desire for grace and peace for the readers, found also in First Peter, is here connected with increasing "through the knowledge of God and of Jesus our Lord." This increased knowledge will result in multiplied grace and peace.

❏ *2 Peter 1:3-11.* The crisis in the church is the threat of heresy. False teachers are denying scriptural truths, even scoffing at the second coming of Christ. Peter begins his letter by reminding his readers of the extraordinary basis for their faith and life. God has called them; they must strive to confirm that call.

Second Peter 1:3-4 provides an introductory statement to the main statement that begins with 1:5. The main thought in this introduction is the gift God has given (granted) to people of faith (us). Notice the characteristics of the gift:

1. the gift is a complete package, providing all that is needed to live a godly life (1:3);

2. it comes through knowledge of God, the One who called us through Jesus to share "his own glory and goodness" (1:3);

3. God's gift provides a protective shield, a means of escaping the life-destroying effects of worldly passions (1:4);

4. it provides the means for sharing God's essential nature (1:4).

God has provided spiritual gifts and knowledge for people of faith. However, additional effort is required on their part (1:5). They need to confirm eagerly their calling and election (1:10).

Verses 5-7 list eight qualities Christians should have in their lives. Each equality promotes acquiring the next.

Faith is the foundation of the Christian life. Without faith it is impossible to please God (Hebrews 11:6).

Goodness is moral power, goodness of life, and strength of Christian character.

Knowledge is the knowledge "of God and of Jesus our Lord" mentioned in 1:2-3.

Self-control is promoted by knowledge of one's self. It involves the mind: Thoughts can be controlled. Self-control also involves the body: Christians can subdue desires, controlling the body by directing it to alternative activities.

HOW TO HANDLE THE CRISIS IN THE CHURCH   **75**

Perseverance is sometimes rendered "patience," sometimes "steadfastness." Perseverance is the ability to endure.

Godliness is a reverent attitude toward God.

Brotherly kindness is love for the other members of the family of God.

Love is a genuine concern for the good and welfare of another person, rather than an emotional feeling.

The person who possesses an abundance of these qualities will be productive in the Christian life, full of love and good works. God saves people for a purpose.

The person who has saving faith but does not add these characteristics to that faith is terribly handicapped (1:9). Shortsighted and forgetful of the cleansing power of Jesus' blood, that person is destined for disaster.

Believers who diligently endeavor to confirm God's call will be so engrossed in the effort that they will have no occasion to stumble (1:10). The reward for the effort will be heaven itself (1:11).

❑ *2 Peter 1:12-15.* The basis of faith is "the knowledge of God and of Jesus our Lord" (1:2). The Christian virtues must be added to faith if believers are to be steadfast and fruitful. The bedrock of the Christian life is the certainty of the truth of the testimony. Peter now turns to that certainty. He wants his readers to keep this true witness in mind.

Peter is determined to leave his readers a permanent reminder (1:12). This letter is that reminder. It is a reminder of truths they already know, but Christians forget under stress and need to be reminded.

The time had come to leave this permanent reminder. Peter was still alive ("in the tent of this body"), but he knew that he was soon to die. His coming death was in fulfillment of Christ's prediction (John 21:18-19). Peter may also have received further revelation from Christ shortly before he wrote this letter (2 Peter 1:14).

❑ *2 Peter 1:16-18.* Peter is emphatic that Christ is no myth. Peter and the other apostles had known to the early Christians the details about the first coming of Jesus Christ.

Jesus came in power. The power Peter had in mind was that which he witnessed on the Mount of Transfiguration (Matthew

17:1-8). He, James, and John also witnessed the majesty of Jesus Christ. They heard a voice from heaven: "This is my Son, whom I love; with him I am well pleased " (Matthew 17:5). This event was a personal experience of the apostle and a historical occurrence on a rock-solid mountain.

❏ *2 Peter 1:19-21.* The coming of Jesus verified the testimony of the prophets.

The readers of Peter's testimony will do well to heed the prophetic witness. This witness is like a lamp in a distant window, guiding travelers through the dark toward their destination.

To keep the prophetic word requires understanding its source. The prophets spoke under the inspiration of the Holy Spirit (1:21). Likewise, the interpretation of Scripture must be by those inspired by the Holy Spirit (1:20).

❏ *2 Peter 2:1-3.* False prophets arose among God's people in Old Testament times (Deuteronomy 13:1-5; Jeremiah 6:13; 28:9; Ezekiel 13:9). Jesus warned against false prophets (Matthew 7:15).

False teachers will arise in the church, Peter writes. They can be identified by their teachings and actions:

1. they subtly bring in ideas of their own that pose a threat to the unity and spiritual health of the church (2:1);

2. they deny the Lord who redeemed them by cleverly twisting the truth about him (2:1);

3. they entice others into sexual immorality, discrediting thereby the way of truth (2:2);

4. they are slyly covetous, using lies to exploit the gullible (2:3).

The downfall of false teachers is as certain as the downfall of the ungodly in the past.

❏ *2 Peter 2:4-10a.* Peter provides examples of deserved destruction on the ungodly:

1. when certain angels sinned, they were cast out of heaven into hell; they went from realms of light to darkest right, there to await the final judgment (2:4; compare Jude 6);

2. the violence of the ancient world resulted in their destruction in the Flood (2:5; compare 1 Peter 3:20);

HOW TO HANDLE THE CRISIS IN THE CHURCH   **77**

3. Sodom and Gomorrah were the epitome of ungodly people; fire from heaven consumed them (2:6).

On the other hand, God rescued "Lot, a righteous man" (2:7).

God did all this in the past. God knows how to save the faithful ones while punishing the ungodly (2:9-10a).

❏ *2 Peter 2:10b-16.* Peter is devastating in his description of the false teachers, so-called Christians. Here is the catalog of their ungodliness:

1. "bold and arrogant, these men are not afraid to slander celestial beings (2:10b);

2. they act like brute animals and will be destroyed like beasts of prey (2:12-13a);

3. they revel and entice others to join them in reveling (2:13b-14);

4. they are under God's curse, like Balaam (2:15-16; Numbers 22–24).

❏ *2 Peter 2:17-22.* False teachers give a false impression to the naive (those "who are just escaping from those who live in error"). They promise a freedom they cannot deliver because they are themselves slaves to corruption. The false teachers will end up worse off than they were before they accepted Jesus Christ as Lord and Savior. They are disgusting.

❏ *2 Peter 3:1-7.* Peter's last concern in this letter is the certainty of the second coming of Christ. Scoffers (false teachers) will

1. appear "in the last days" (3:3);

2. be motivated by their own evil desires, not by the Spirit of God (3:3-4);

3. deliberately ignore the power and certainty of the word of God (3:5), which they contradict.

❏ *2 Peter 3:8-10.* Peter provides the response to scoffers:

1. God does not mark time the way people do (3:8; Psalm 90:4);

2. the grace of God is not slow in coming (3:9), for God is not willing that any perish but that all shall come to repentance;

3. that day will come like a thief in the night (3:10), unexpected and catastrophic.

❏ *2 Peter 3:11-18.* To await "the day of the Lord," Christians should

1. anticipate that day (3:12);
2. hasten its coming by living holy and godly lives (3:11);
3. look for a new creation in which righteousness and they will be at home (3:13);
4. be zealous to be holy and at peace, so they can be found that way when Jesus comes (3:14);
5. appreciate the patience of God for the salvation of others (3:15a).

The apostolic witness includes the letters of Paul. He also urged godly living and preparation for Christ's return.

Ignorant and unstable people twist the Scriptures, including Paul's words, giving them false explanations. This false teaching will bring disaster on their heads (and on the heads of those who are gullible).

Peter closes the letter without the expected conclusion (as in 1 Peter 5:12-14). He wraps it up neatly, however, returning to his opening thoughts on "the grace and knowledge of our Lord and Savior Jesus Christ" (3:18). Peter had seen Christ's glory on the mountaintop. Jesus Christ deserved that glory then. He deserves it now and forever.

DIMENSION THREE:
WHAT DOES THE BIBLE MEAN TO ME?

1. The Gospel accounts present Jesus as a historical person (2 Peter 1:16-18). How important is the historicity of these accounts to you personally? How important is it to the life of the church?

2. Some Christians are obsessed with the second coming of Christ. To what degree has the discussion in 2 Peter 3 helped you have a realistic view of the Second Coming?

If we walk in the light, as he is in the light,
we have fellowship with one another (1:7).

—— 10 ——
The Basis of
Christian Fellowship
1 John 1–2

DIMENSION ONE:
WHAT DOES THE BIBLE SAY?

Answer these questions by reading 1 John 1

1. With what physical senses had John experienced contact with the Word of life? (1:1)

2. What did John want the readers to share? (1:3)

3. What benefits does walking in the light bring to the Christian? (1:7)

Answer these questions by reading 1 John 2

4. How may Christians be sure that they know Christ? (2:3)

5. How can a person know that he or she is in the light? (2:9-10)

6. For what three things did John commend the young men to whom he wrote? (2:14b)

7. What is the evidence that the last hour has come? (2:18)

8. How can an antichrist be identified? (2:22c)

9. What is promised to those who remain in the Son and in the Father? (2:24b-25)

10. How should those who remain in Christ act when he comes? (2:28)

DIMENSION TWO: WHAT DOES THE BIBLE MEAN?

❏ *The Writer.* This lesson is the first of three that will deal with the writings of John. We assume that they were written by the apostle John. He was the son of Zebedee and a companion of Jesus.

We cannot be positive that John wrote these letters. The writer is not named in any of the three epistles. Early in the history of the church, however, the writer of the letters was thought to be John. The writings of some of the early church fathers reflect ideas found in the writings of John and include phrases that sound almost like quotations.

We can find many similarities of thought and word combinations between the Gospel of John and these letters. However, we associate the Fourth Gospel with John because of tradition too. He does not name himself as the writer.

If John did not write the letters, then an "Elder John" might have done so. That suggestion is based on the words *the elder* that are found in the opening verses of Second and Third John. He would have been a person who was a follower of the writer of the Gospel of John.

For our purposes, however, we will assume that the apostle John is our writer, based on the early testimony of the church fathers.

❑ *Time and Place of Writing.* The three letters were written about the same time as the Gospel of John. The time was approximately A.D. 90–100. The general view is that these books were written from Ephesus. That is because of the tradition that the apostle John spent his later years there, supervising the churches in that major city and in the region round about. This region is the location of the seven churches to whom the letters in the Book of Revelation are addressed (Revelation 2–3).

The writer seems to have been very old when he wrote, for he addresses his readers, young and old alike, as "dear children" and "my dear children." According to tradition, the apostle John was the last of the apostles of Jesus to die. That was near the end of the first century. So these letters form a part of the last apostolic witness.

❑ *Persons Addressed.* The letters of Paul usually name the persons or churches for whom they were intended. First John does not name those to whom it was sent. This letter is a general communication to Christians wherever they might be found. Because Christians today fit into that group, the letter is particularly meaningful for us.

❑ *Purpose of First John.* The purpose, as stated in the first four verses of the letter, is to declare the "Word of life," the gospel of Jesus Christ, in order that the writer and the readers may have fellowship with God and Christ and with one another. The word of life is the foundation for the fellowship. The fellowship will help all to experience the fullest joy.

The letter was also written to alert believers to the dangers that might threaten the fellowship with God in Christ. False teachers (antichrists) were enticing believers to believe lies about the true nature of the Christ. They were encouraging Christians to live lives of selfishness, fulfilling ungodly passions rather than keeping the commandments of Jesus Christ.

The warnings of John to the first readers of this letter are best understood against the threat of these false teachers. They were a part of the Gnostic movement within the church. Gnostic thought had to be fought by the church beginning in apostolic times and through the second century A.D.

Gnostic comes from the Greek work *gnosis,* meaning "knowledge." The Gnostic teachers claimed to have special knowledge that was beyond and superior to the testimony of the apostles about Jesus. They held a nonbiblical view of the origin of the world, of the nature of God, of the nature of humans, and of the nature of the Christ. They denied that the Christ was born of a woman and fully human. They distinguished between the spirit as good and the body as actually evil. Therefore, they denied the bodily resurrection of Jesus Christ.

Gnostic teaching involved much more than we can discuss here. Bible dictionaries and histories of early Christianity will provide more information. We should note, though, that gnosticism was an element in the church only at first. Believers in Gnostic doctrine soon were expelled from orthodox groups. The movement to separate those who believed in the historical testimony of the gospel from Gnostics was underway when John wrote his works that are part of our New Testament.

❏ *Organization of First John.* This book seems to be a collection of thoughts rather than the logical development of an idea we usually find in biblical books. We have arranged our study to focus on fellowship as the main theme.

❏ *1 John 1:1-4.* The grammar of these opening verses is not easy to understand. What is being said, though, is similar to the first few verses of John's Gospel. *The Contemporary English Version* may help you understand the passage:

"The Word that gives life was from the beginning, and this is the one our message is about. Our ears have heard, our own eyes have seen, and our hands touched this Word. The one who gives life appeared! We saw it happen, and we are witnesses to what we have seen. Now we are telling you about this eternal life that was with the Gather and appeared to us. We are telling you what we have seen and heard, so that you may share in this life with us. And we share in it with the Father and with his Son Jesus Christ." (1 John 1:1-3, *Contemporary English Version,* CEV).

The essential points are

1. Jesus, the Christ (Messiah) was a real person; the apostolic testimony was based on personal experience;

2. their testimony, when received and believed, is the basis for sharing in the eternal life with the Father, the Son, and all who believe.

This sharing (fellowship) in eternal life is presently going on and is not just in the future. That is why John and his readers can have full, complete joy.

❑ *1 John 1:5–2:29.* The core of this letter is the subject of fellowship. Fellowship is sharing something in common. What is shared here is eternal life. It is shared "with the Father," "with his Son, Jesus Christ," and with those who believe in Christ. What they share in communion makes them a community. The community is called the church. The church is the called-out people of God.

Believers are described as "in Christ" (2 Corinthians 5:17). Believers are Christ's, and Christ is God's person (1 Corinthians 3:23). Christ dwells in the hearts of believers (Ephesians 3:17), and "Christ in you [is] the hope of glory" (Colossians 1:27). This is the fellowship.

The testimony about Jesus is the basis of the fellowship. John lists five conditions for maintaining the fellowship.

❑ *1 John 1:5-10.* God is light; that is, God is pure and holy. To walk in the light is to not walk in darkness (1 John 1:6), enjoy the fellowship (1:7), and be purified of all sin (1:7). The purifying is by the blood of Jesus. Confession of our sins must precede the purifying. Purifying applies to everyone, because all have sinned. To say differently is to lie.

❑ *1 John 2:1-6.* Baptized believers are to be dead to sin (Romans 6:1-4). They are buried with Christ in baptism to rise to walk in newness of life. They share in Christ's resurrection. One cannot be a slave to sin and a servant of God's. A Christian will not follow the way of the world, but all believers will slip and fall on the narrow way once in a while. So John speaks here of not living in sin. He also speaks of that occasional, single act that is sin.

When a person in the joyous fellowship sins, that threatens to pollute that person's relationship with God. The sin throws a shadow across the One who is light. But the person who so sins has a defense lawyer (advocate) before the heavenly throne. Jesus Christ comes to the defense; his shed blood obliterates the sin and removes the shadow (2:1-2).

By God's marvelous love and grace, Jesus has expiated (paid the price for forgiveness for) the sins of the whole world. This priceless gift is available and effective only for those who accept it by accepting him.

Those who take pleasure in keeping Jesus Christ's commandments can be certain that they "know him." Knowing him is another way of speaking of the fellowship the believer has with Christ. But the one who says "I know him" and finds no joy in keeping Christ's commandments lies to others and deceives himself or herself. The Gnostics did this. They claimed special knowledge of Christ but ignored his commandments (2:4-6). The true disciple will follow in the footsteps of Jesus.

❑ *1 John 2:7-11.* James spoke of the royal law: "If you really keep the royal law found in Scripture, 'Love your neighbor as yourself,' you are doing right" (James 2:8). That is, we are to love one another. This royal law is the old command summarized by Jesus in Matthew 22:34-40. The old command has not been changed, but to it has been added another phrase.

To love is to have a genuine concern for the well-being of the other person. Unconcern is the same as hate. To teach or do something that causes another member of the fellowship to stumble shows unconcern. This lack of love marks a person as one who walks in darkness rather than in the light of the apostolic testimony.

❑ *1 John 2:12-17.* Again John speaks directly to his readers. The way in which he addresses them indicates that what he says is for all believers in all times and in all places. What he says for one, whether old or young, applies to all. They know God; that is, they have a relationship with God. That relationship will naturally lead to having God's word abide in them.

Verse 15 reminds us of Jesus' teaching in the Sermon on the Mount: "No one can serve two masters. Either he will hate the one and love the other, or he will be devoted to the one and despise the other. You cannot serve both God and money" (Matthew 6:24). *The world* is a general term that covers the cravings (evil desire) of sinful persons, the lust of the eyes, and the boasting of what a person has and does as mentioned by John in verse 16.

Those in fellowship with God and Jesus Christ have eternal life. Those whose only fellowship is with this world are bound to end up unsatisfied, for this world passes away. Joy is much more satisfying than fulfilling lusts.

❑ *1 John 2:18-29.* "The last hour" refers to the period in which the forces of righteousness confront the forces of evil. This period began when Jesus came to establish the kingdom of God. God has spoken his final message to the world in his Son, Jesus Christ (Hebrews 1:2). The spiritual conflict will continue until the second coming of Christ. The struggle for righteousness is carried on by the church, for it is the body of Christ.

For each person who is in the fellowship of the redeemed (the church), "the last hour" is during that person's lifetime. When Christians die, they cease from their labors. The end time has ended for them.

That the end time is at hand is evident from the antichrists. Every generation has some antichrists. They begin within the church. They pervert the testimony on which the fellowship is based. They do this by holding unscriptural views of Jesus, thus denying to some degree that Jesus is the Christ, as foretold by the prophets and testified to by the apostles (2:22-23). These views cause disunity and division in the church. Then the antichrists may go their way, taking the vulnerable with them.

Such were the Gnostics and their followers in the time of this letter.

The anointing of the Holy Spirit and adherence to the true testimony will counteract the spirit of the antichrist (2:20-21, 24-25). By remaining in the word, believers can be certain that they remain in Christ. Remaining in Christ means continuing in the fellowship, and that is eternal life. External life is experienced now to a degree; it will be experienced fully in the future when Christ comes again.

To emphasize what he said earlier, John repeats the same ideas in 2:26-27. Again, in 2:28, John urges his readers to "continue in him." Those who do will not have been deceived by the liars who deny the Father and the Son. Those who are not deceived will have confidence when Christ comes. They will not shrink back in fear, for they have been enjoying the fellowship before his coming. Their joy will simply increase. Such people reflect the genetic connections to Jesus that come with the new birth. They reflect the family trait of doing right.

DIMENSION THREE: WHAT DOES THE BIBLE MEAN TO ME?

1. How can you apply the direction "walk as Jesus did" (2:6) to your life?

2. How do you understand "the cravings of sinful man," "the lust of the eyes," and "the boasting of what has and does" (2:16)? To what extent are these negative forces at work in the church in our time?

*Everyone who believes that Jesus is the Christ
is born of God, and everyone who loves the father
loves his child as well (5:1).*

—— **11** ——

*Fellowship in
the Family of God*

1 John 3–5

DIMENSION ONE:
WHAT DOES THE BIBLE SAY?

Answer these questions by reading 1 John 3

1. What two things can God's children be sure of when Christ appears? (3:2b)

2. How can the children of God be distinguished from "the children of the devil"? (3:7-10)

3. In what practical way can Christians show love "with actions and in truth"? (3:17-18)

4. What are the two basic commands of God to Christians? (3:23)

5. How can we determine who has the Spirit of God and who has the spirit of the antichrist? (4:2-3)

6. What two things did God do that show God's love for us? (4:9-10)

7. Why is love a valid test of the love a person has for God? (4:20-21)

Answer these questions by reading 1 John 5

8. What is the content of the faith that overcomes the world? (5:4-5)

9. What three witnesses testify that God gave us eternal life in Jesus Christ? (5:6-8)

10. John describes the two types of sin. What does he call these two types? (5:16-17)

11. If "the whole world is under the control of the evil one," why is the one born of God not in the power of the evil one? (5:18-19)

12. Of what temptation in particular does John warn Christians at the end of his letter? (5:21)

DIMENSION TWO: WHAT DOES THE BIBLE MEAN?

Our first lesson on First John showed how the theme of fellowship ties the varied parts of the letter together in a loose way. The conditions of the fellowship with God and with Jesus Christ are presented in Lesson 10. They are to walk in the light, to walk in the footsteps of Jesus, to pass the test of love, to know God and keep God's commands, and to shun the antichrists while remaining in Christ. The rest of First John describes the fellowship in terms of a family relationship. Before John closes the letter, he spotlights a number of facets of the fellowship.

❑ *1 John 3:1-3.* John, we assume, was a young man when he first met Jesus (Matthew 4:18-22). He was as close to Jesus as any of the disciples. John saw all the events of the Crucifixion. He visited the empty tomb with Peter. He was in the upper room when Jesus made his appearance after the resurrection. He stood on the Mount of Olives and heard the final words of Jesus just before Jesus' ascension. All these things happened long before John wrote this letter. And yet, even as an old man, he was still amazed at what God had done in Christ.

In 3:1, we can sense John's emotions. He wanted his readers to share in his wonder. People who were alienated from the Creator are now a part of the family of God!

The idea of Christians being part of the family of God was first expressed in 2:29. "Everyone who does what is right" can claim the family relationship. All this is possible thanks to the love of God.

The Greek word used to identify God's love is *agape*. *Agape* describes a genuine concern for the welfare of others. Such love is not selfish or self-seeking. The most accurate description of that kind of love exists in 1 Corinthians 13. But even Paul's words cannot do justice to God's love. God had such a concern for a world lost in sin that God sent the best heaven could offer to save it (John 3:16).

Children of God can expect the world to treat them like the rest of the family, God and Jesus (3:1c). The world rejected Jesus, reviled him, and persecuted him. It did not understand him; it will not understand us. The family connection, however, is worth any worldly rejection. When Jesus Christ comes again, in the resurrection of believers, God's children will be like God's first-born Son—pure and worthy of heaven. This knowledge gives them confidence and hope (3:2-3).

Imagine how encouraging these words were to the Christians to whom John first wrote. They were being buffeted by persecutions and badgered by false teachers.

❏ *1 John 3:4-10.* God's children seek to be pure. They purify themselves by taking advantage of the finished work of Jesus (3:5-6). They purify their souls by obedience to the truth (1 Peter 1:22). They are easily distinguished from the children of the devil. The children of the devil make a practice of sinning, of lawlessness (3:4, 8a).

The children of God were once children of the devil. They were once separated from Christ, strangers to the covenants of promise, having no hope, and without God in the world (Ephesians 2:12). But Christ came to destroy the works of the devil. he came to destroy the desire to sin and the effects of sin. By faith in Christ and confidence in his finished work, believers "who once were far away have been brought near through the blood of Christ" (Ephesians 2:13).

Just as genetics in human families give the members certain traits—color of the eyes, height, shape of the nose, and so on—so the children of God and the children of the devil can be identified by the family characteristics (3:9-10). God's children do right and love the other members of the family. The devil's children do not do right and do not love others.

The distinction John is making is between the usual practices of people. The children of the devil may occasionally do good, but normally they act selfishly. The children of God may occasionally sin, but normally they act in selfless love.

❏ *1 John 3:11-18.* Members of the fellowship of God's family are to love one another in a selfless way. Cain is an example of one who did not act lovingly toward another family member.

We have no exact knowledge of why Cain's sacrifice was not accepted (Genesis 4:3-7). The text in Genesis indicates that he failed to "do what is right," and sin was lurking at the door. Here we are told that he murdered his brother "because his own actions were evil." Cain's sinful attitude ended in a murderous action. That is the way the world operates. Selfishness leads to damaging actions against others.

To live selfishly and sinfully is to abide in death (3:14). Death is separation. Death can include separation from other people. Death can also be separation from God. That seems to be the meaning here, for the opposite of abiding in death is to have eternal life. Eternal life, of course, is the same as being in the fellowship mentioned at the beginning of the letter. It is being in the family of God.

The test of family membership is not in what is said but in what is done (3:16-18). Christ gave his life for us; we should lay down our lives for members of the family of God. Here laying down our lives means sharing the world's goods we may possess with God's children whom we see in need. This kind of sharing is loving "with actions and in truth." God's children love one another with generous actions rather than with empty words.

❏ *1 John 3:19-24.* Most sensitive Christians have felt twinges of guilt over something they have thought or done. Daily we make moral judgments and act on them. We cannot always be certain we have walked "as Jesus did" (2:6).

John was aware of this. He knew that sometimes "our hearts condemn us" (3:20); our conscience bothers us. Here he encourages his readers. The "This" of 3:19 refers to loving "with actions and in truth." If this is our way of life, then even when our conscience is troubled, we can have confidence that we are still God's children. We can still pray confidently, for "if we confess our sins, he is faithful and just and will forgive us our sins and purify us from all unrighteousness" (1:9).

God's children naturally try to keep God's commands. They are to believe in God's Son and to love one another. The ties that bind God's family together are strong. God will abide in God's children and they in God (John 14:23). We know that God abides in us by the Holy Spirit that God has given to us.

The continuing presence of the Holy Spirit was promised to the disciples by Jesus. He made the promise in the upper room on the night in which he was betrayed (John 14:15-26; 15:26-27; 16:7-13). The Spirit came in power on the day of Pentecost. On that occasion Peter assured all who accepted his testimony about Christ that they would receive the gift of the Holy Spirit. The Spirit is a gift to baptized believers (Acts 2:38).

❏ *1 John 4:1-6.* In this world children of the devil and false teachers need to be identified by Christians. The children of the devil can be identified by their lack of loving deeds. The false prophets can be identified by the spirit in which they teach. (*Prophet* here is the equivalent of *teacher.*)

God's children have been given the Spirit of God. They are to "test the spirits" of the teachers to see if they are of God. Some who appear to be godly teachers actually have the spirit of the antichrist. (John probably has in mind here the Gnostic teachers. See Lesson 10 for information on the Gnostics.) Paul once warned the Christians at Corinth in a similar way. He wrote: "And no wonder, for Satan himself masquerades as an angel of light. It is not surprising, then, if his servants masquerade as servants of righteousness" (2 Corinthians 11:14-15a).

How can the false teachers who have the spirit of the antichrist be detected? How can they be distinguished from teachers in whom the Holy Spirit abides? John lists three tests: (1) Do they confess that Jesus Christ has come in the flesh? That is, do they accept and teach that he was human and the Messiah promised in the Hebrew scriptures? (2) Do they speak what the world likes to hear, the cravings of sinful persons, the lust of the eyes, and the boasting about what a person has and does (2:16)? (3) Do they hear (accept) the testimony of John and the other apostles? If the answers to the tests are no, yes, no, then they are the spirit of error and of the antichrist.

On the other hand, God's children share God's Spirit. Teachers who have the spirit of truth confess that Jesus Christ has come in the flesh, speak the truth, and listen to the apostolic witness.

❑ *1 John 4:7–5:17*. The last part of First John emphasizes a number of important Christian concepts.

❑ *1 John 4:7-21*. Children of God should reflect the main family feature—love. God is the source of that characteristic (4:7-8). God is also the example of love (4:9-13). The evidence that God lives in us is in how we love one another. This love is the evidence of the work of the Holy Spirit in the life of a person.

The love of God for us and our love for others in the family of God is a source of confidence now and hope for the future (4:14-21). We are Christ's and Christ is God's. We have no fear of judgment when we love like God loves. Proof that we love God, whom we have not seen, is in how we love the other family members, whom we do see.

❑ *1 John 5:1-5*. Faith in Jesus Christ and as the Son of God makes possible our becoming a part of the family of God. Love for the children of God is evidence that we remain God's children and that we have overcome the world.

❑ *1 John 5:6-12*. God has provided three witnesses that Jesus is the Christ: (1) the water (of his baptism, John 1:19-34), (2) the blood (of his atonement, John 19:34), and (3) the Spirit (of truth, John 15:26). Eternal life comes by accepting the unanimous testimony of the three. Then the one who believes becomes a bearer of the testimony too.

❑ 1 John 5:13-21. As he nears the end of his letter, John again provides an encouraging word. Those in the fellowship, in the family of God, should be confident in their faith and in their prayers. As family members, they will pray according to the will of God (5:14). A part of a loving concern for the other members of the family is to pray for them.

We cannot be sure which sin "leads to death" (5:16). Probably it was a rejection of the apostolic testimony and a departure from the family of God; that is, becoming an apostate, one who stands apart.

But a secure wall is cast up about the children of God. Their relationship assures believers that the evil one cannot touch them (5:18). The whole world is in the power of the evil one—it is his domain—but the one born of God is kept by the Son ("the one who was born of God").

Verse 20 brings the reader back to where the letter began (1:1-3). The fellowship that is eternal life is established by receiving the testimony of "we/us," the apostles. The Son of God, to whom they testify, is the way, the truth, and the life. Those who are in the fellowship have understanding. No Gnostic teacher can provide any secret knowledge that will result in knowing the true God and receiving eternal life. That knowledge and that eternal life come through God's Son Jesus Christ.

An idol is any substitute for the true God. John's final appeal is couched in the fatherly expression we have heard so frequently, "Dear children." Guard yourselves against every false god.

DIMENSION THREE:
WHAT DOES THE BIBLE MEAN TO ME?

1. The miracle of modern media and the low cost of bulk mail have combined in our time to flood us with information on human needs at home and abroad. How do you deal responsibly and in love with the appeals for help you receive?

2. What positive statements in First John struck a responsive chord in your heart? Share these with your study group or with a personal friend.

This is love: that we walk in obedience to his commands (2 John 6).

—— 12 ——
Two Personal Letters From John
2 John and 3 John

DIMENSION ONE:
WHAT DOES THE BIBLE SAY?

Answer these questions by reading 2 John

1. How does the writer identify himself? (verse 1)

2. Identify the main word used by the writer in the salutation. (verses 1-3)

3. Why was the writer joyful about news he received concerning the "chosen lady and her children"? (verse 4)

4. Above all else, what did the writer want the readers to do? (verses 5-6)

5. What is the identifying mark of a deceiver and the anti-christ? (verse 7)

6. Why shouldn't a Christian receive into the house nor greet someone who does not continue in the teaching of Christ? (verses 10-11)

7. Why is this letter so short? (verse 12)

Answer these questions by reading 3 John

8. How did the elder know that all was well with the soul of Gaius? (verses 2-3)

9. In the elder's opinion, what is an especially worthy thing for a Christian to do? (verses 5-6)

10. What specific things did Diotrephes do that the elder condemned? (verses 9-10)

11. Why did the elder commend Demetrius? (verse 12)

12. Why is the elder's letter to Gaius so brief? (verses 13-14)

DIMENSION TWO:
WHAT DOES THE BIBLE MEAN?

Most Bible scholars believe there is a close relationship among First John, Second John, and Third John. You may want to review the discussion in Lesson 10. Briefly, however, the matters of writer, date, and place can be summarized as follows.

1. *Writer.* These three letters do not name the writer, but the first paragraph of First John indicates that it was written by an apostle. The writer testifies that he heard, saw, and touched the "Word of life." That expression connects First John with the beginning of the Gospel of John (1:1, 14).

Although the Gospel of John does not name its writer, certain incidents and expressions in that book indicate that the apostle John wrote it. Similarities of expression and style strongly suggest that John was the writer of the Gospel and the three letters. This inner evidence is supported also by the weight of Christian tradition.

2. *Date.* The letters and the Gospel were written about the same time, A.D. 90–100. John seems to have been quite old when he wrote the letters, for he addresses young and old alike as "dear children."

3. *Place.* Tradition places the apostle John in Ephesus during the latter years of his life. He apparently supervised the churches in that region. At one point he was exiled to the Isle of Patmos, off the coast of modern Turkey (Revelation 1:9).

❑ *Relationship of First, Second, and Third John.* First John is not addressed to a particular church or individual. It was probably intended as a general letter to the church at large. Second John is addressed to "the chosen lady and her children." Third John is a personal letter, addressed to Gaius. He was a Christian friend of John's who lived in a place not mentioned.

First John and Second John are similar in style and expression. The word *antichrist* appears in both letters. Second John has been described as the specific application of the teachings of First John. Love and truth are emphasized in all three letters. Second and Third John were written by the "elder."

These close relationships among the letters make the study of all three at the same time useful. Together they give us a sense of the way in which the longest living apostle encouraged and taught the church a half century after it began.

❏ *Concerns of Second John.* The writer emphasizes "the truth" in this short letter. He also warns of the deceivers who are traveling about. They are not to be shown hospitality, for they deny the truth of the gospel, that Jesus Christ came in the flesh.

❏ *2 John 1–3.* The writer calls himself "the elder" at the beginning of the letter. This term takes the place of the personal name of the writer usually found at the beginning of letters in the New Testament.

Elder means an older person. In biblical times older members of a community were respected and looked to for wise counsel and leadership. But the word also had a more exact usage. It could mean a person with authority. Elders in ancient Israel helped Moses direct the Israelites (Numbers 11:16). We also hear of elders in Bethlehem in the time of the judges of Israel (Ruth 4:2).

In Jesus' time a council of seventy elders, called the Sanhedrin, governed the religious affairs of the Jews in Jerusalem. Jewish synagogues across the Roman Empire were likewise directed by elders.

The churches that Paul established had similar directors called elders (Acts 14:23). That elders were the authorities in the early churches is evident from 1 Peter 5:1-5. Peter even calls himself "a fellow elder" (1 Peter 5:1). So we can understand why John would use *elder* as his title rather than *apostle.*

Just as the identity of *the elder* has been much discussed, so has the identity of *the chosen lady.* The Greek phrase means "an excellent lady of superior rank and character." She may have been a devout Christian who supported the church with her wealth and influence. Or *lady* may mean church. The church is pictured as a woman, the "bride of Christ," in Ephesians

5:23-32. If *lady* means church here, then *her children* means the members of the church. We have adopted that view for this study.

In his opening John says he loves the church "in the truth." This expression can mean that he "truly" loved the church. It can also mean that he loved those to whom he wrote because they shared in the truth of the gospel.

Jesus said, "I am the way and the truth and the life" (John 14:6). All who abide in that truth love "the chosen lady," the church. To love Christ is to love the church, for the church is the body of Christ (Ephesians 1:22-23).

Since Jesus is the truth and since "Christ in you [is] the hope of glory" (Colossians 1:27), John can speak of the truth that abides forever in believers. The reality of the love of "God the Father" and "Jesus Christ, the Father's Son" is the source of confidence for John. He is certain that he and his readers will continue to enjoy grace, mercy, and peace.

❑ *2 John 4–6.* The elder began the letter with a positive emphasis on love and truth. He builds on that emphasis by encouraging "the lady" to follow love and to beware of those who despise the truth, the deceivers.

Apparently the elder visited the lady and her children and found some of them following the truth of God's will and word. He writes to express his deep pleasures at this.

His joy has a sad note, however. Only some of the children were following the truth. Perhaps the others had fallen under the influence of the deceivers he mentions in verse 7.

Verses 5-6 contain a strong plea. He asks that the lady walk in love. Walking in love means following the commandments of Jesus Christ. These verses echo 1 John 4:7, "Dear friends, let us love one another, for love comes from God. Everyone who loves has been born of God and knows God." This love requires actions as well as words: "Dear children, let us not love with words or tongue but with actions and in truth" (1 John 3:18).

❑ *2 John 7–11.* Christian love is not blind. A believer must follow love while being aware of deceivers. "Many deceivers, who do not acknowledge Jesus Christ as coming in the flesh, have gone out into the world." This echoes 1 John 4:1b: "Many false prophets have gone out into the world." These deceivers were once counted as true Christians, but they held unscriptural ideas about Jesus. They could not accept that God had come in the flesh, that Jesus was truly human.

We are not told in Second John exactly what these deceivers thought about Jesus. We do know that in the second century A.D. the first great crisis in the church came. It is called the "Gnostic crisis." Read the description of this crisis in Lesson 10.

Whatever the exact views of the deceivers were, they were not the truth. John know the truth about Jesus. He had spoken with him, touched him, listened to his teachings, and seen what he did. John had stood at the foot of the cross and knew that Jesus shed his human blood in his death. John was certain that Jesus had come in the flesh.

Anyone who taught any other view about Jesus was a deceiver. All deceivers are antichrists. Everyone who claims to be a believer and who does not confess that Jesus Christ has come in the flesh is against Christ (1 John 4:3). That person is a servant of the chief deceiver, the devil (Revelation 20:10).

Verse 8 sounds as if the elder is writing to a church, for he says, "Watch out." Christians are not to be selfish or self-centered. They are to build themselves up on their most holy faith (Jude 20). They should guard against being taken in by the false views of the deceivers. Anyone who goes on ahead, away from the true doctrine of Christ, is without God.

In order to win a full reward, a Christian should be careful not to assist deceivers. Do not offer hospitality to one who professes to be a Christian but who rejects the truth that Jesus came in the flesh. To help such an antichrist evangelist is to share in his wicked work. Thus the elder warns the elect lady.

❏ *2 John 12–13.* The words of encouragement, warning, and exhortation have ended. The letter is short, probably so that it would fit on a single piece of papyrus, the writing paper of the time.

The elder hoped to expand on the letter in a face-to-face conversation. He hoped to visit "the chosen lady," which would be a deep pleasure for both of them. In the meantime, his fellow Christians in the church where he was sent their greetings with his.

❑ *3 John 1–4.* The familiar time *the elder* opens Third John. Gaius, who receives the letter, is loved in the truth by the writer, just as was "the chosen lady" in Second John. Since Gaius is mentioned by name, this letter is more personal than First John or Second John.

Verse 2 expresses the writer's desire that his dear friend would experience good health and prosperity. He knew that Gaius was spiritually healthy and flourishing because visiting Christians who had arrived from Gaius told him so (verse 3). They testified that Gaius was following the truth. Of course, this report brought great joy to the elder, just as a similar report in Second John brought him great joy (2 John 4).

❑ *3 John 5–8.* Gaius practiced Christian hospitality toward traveling teachers. John commends him for this service. This hospitality is evidence of his loyalty and love for the truth. Gaius's generous help was known in many places, for these traveling teachers spoke of it wherever they went.

In verse 6, John encourages Gaius to send such faithful travelers on their way. Gaius was to provide for their needs after they left his home, enough so that they could make it to their next destination without difficulty. This means of support for "circuit riding" preachers followed the pattern established by Jesus (Matthew 10:5-15).

The teachers/preachers sent out by John, it seems, were not to look to non-Christians for support. God's people ought to take care of one another. Hospitality provided to faithful missionaries and people who are traveling for the Lord's business is something Christians ought to do. People who extend such hospitality are fellow workers in the truth.

❑ *3 John 9–10.* Gaius is an example of proper conduct toward traveling teachers. Diotrephes is a negative example. John had written to the church of which Diotrephes seems to have been a leader. But Diotrephes refused to heed the contents of the letter from the elder. He "loves to be first."

John planned to visit the church over which Diotrephes had major control. (Perhaps John's advanced age made him state his plan to visit with an *if.*) Then John would confront the church with what Diotrephes had been saying and doing (verse 10).

Diotrephes was rejecting John's authority. He was refusing hospitality to the brothers who came from John. Diotrephes also prevented other members of the congregation from showing the visitors hospitality. Even more, Diotrephes would excommunicate members of the congregation who hosted travelers who came from John.

❑ *3 John 11–12.* Demetrius may have been a traveling teacher. Possibly he carried the letter from John to Gaius. At any rate, Demetrius is recommended to Gaius as an example of a good person. He is described in contrast to the bad example of Diotrephes. John encourages his dear friend, Gaius, to imitate the good person rather than the bad. Everyone recognized that Demetrius was faithful to the truth. His good character and conduct were evidence that his life was based on the truth. Not least, the testimony of John for Demetrius was completely positive. No one could ask for a better endorsement.

❑ *3 John 13–14.* The elder closes his letter to Gaius in almost the same words as in Second John. He hopes to see him face to face soon.

The elder also prays for God's peace for his friend. Those with John send greetings to Gaius, whose hospitality is so well-known. Perhaps some of them had lodged with him on their travels.

Finally, John asks that his greetings and those of his associates be given to all their friends where Gaius lives. Blessed be the tie that binds the hearts of Christians in love. Distance is no barrier to such ties.

DIMENSION THREE:
WHAT DOES THE BIBLE MEAN TO ME?

1. How important is the doctrine of Christ—that Jesus came in the flesh—to you? How important is it to the existence of the church?

2. In Third John the readers are encouraged to show hospitality to the brothers, especially strangers. What are some attitudes about receiving guests in our homes today that hinder our being hospitable? What can and should the church do to encourage the members to be hospitable toward visiting Christian strangers?

*But you, dear friends, build yourselves up
in your most holy faith, ... keep
yourselves in God's love (Jude 20–21).*

—— 13 ——
The Book of Jude
Jude

DIMENSION ONE:
WHAT DOES THE BIBLE SAY?

Answer these questions by reading Jude

1. How does Jude describe his relationship to Jesus and to James? (verse 1)

2. What three words describe the people to whom Jude writes? (verse 1)

3. What three blessings does Jude pray for his readers? (verse 2)

4. What is the specific reason Jude writes to his Christian readers? (verse 3)

5. What two actions are the godless persons guilty of? (verse 4)

6. In verses 5-7, Jude reminds his readers of God's judgment on three groups who were unbelieving and immoral. Who are these groups?

7. The men mentioned in verse 8 are guilty of three acts worthy of condemnation. List those acts.

8. What act have these men committed that even Michael the archangel would not commit? (verses 9-10)

9. What examples from nature does Jude use to describe the men he condemns? (verses 12-13)

10. According to Enoch, why is the Lord to execute judgment on the godless? (verses 14-16)

11. Of what particular prediction of the apostles does Jude remind his readers? (verses 17-18)

12. What action words does Jude use to urge his readers on in the faith? (verses 20-21)

13. What actions does Jude recommend toward weak Christians? (verses 22-23)

DIMENSION TWO:
WHAT DOES THE BIBLE MEAN?

The Book of Jude is the last of the General Letters. Most of the books in the group are addressed to Christians in general. The opening verse of Jude identifies the writer, but no specific person or church is named as the intended reader or readers.

We may assume, then, that Jude intended for Christians in a number of churches to read the letter. Apparently the problems he discusses were widespread in the churches in the time in which he wrote. What could be written to one church could be written to all. Despite the problems in the churches, Jude saw the members as loved by God.

Jude's concern about the problems in the beloved churches was the reason for his letter. Influential teachers were rejecting the authority of apostolic teaching. They denied essential truths about Jesus Christ. They made light of serious matters. They established themselves as authorities based on their dreamings. They engaged in immoral sex and unnatural lust. These teachers' influence and teaching was swaying the immature and unstable among the Christians. They apparently pushed their views, causing dissension and disunity among the believers. Jude wrote to condemn all this ungodliness.

No one knows exactly when the letter was written. The problems suggest, however, that it was toward the end of the first century A.D. But worldliness was a problem in some churches even in the time of Paul, before A.D. 70. The letter gives us some idea of the continuing conflict between those who accepted the testimony of the apostles and those who sought to modify it by their own views. This struggle was between orthodoxy and heresy.

Besides giving us a sense of the struggles in the church between the godly and the ungodly, the letter provides encouragement to the faithful to vigorously defend the faith. The letter provides specific instructions to enable believers to keep themselves in the love of God and the hope of the gospel of Jesus Christ.

❑ *Jude 1–2.* The writer identifies himself in relation to Jesus and to James. Jesus had a brother named James and another named Jude (Judas). Two other brothers, Simon and Joseph, and some sisters of Jesus are mentioned in Matthew 13:55-56a.) Whether Jude is the brother of Jesus has been argued by scholars. The matter has not been settled to everyone's satisfaction, but until proved otherwise, we can assume that the writer was a younger brother of Jesus as well as of James.

The letter is addressed to "those who have been called." This phrase refers to Christians. They are the called-out people of God. They have been "called . . . out of darkness into his wonderful light" (1 Peter 2:9). They have heard and responded to the gospel call.

The words *grace* and *peace* often appear in the opening of New Testament letters. Here *mercy* and *love* are mentioned along with *peace*. All three words are related to God. Jude could have written, "May the mercy of God, the peace of God, and the love of God be multiplied to you." Jude obviously had a deep love and concern for the church.

❑ *Jude 3–4.* Jude wanted to write about the salvation that he and his readers had in common. Instead, a problem in the church moved him to urge them to fight for the faith. The faith is the content of the gospel, that is, that God is in Christ reconciling the world to himself.

Not only does the faith consist of the stories about Jesus, it also consists of the meaning of what Jesus did for believers. The faith thus includes precious promises, such as abundant life now and life eternal. But the faith also consists of commands to be obeyed. As Jesus said, "Why do you call me 'Lord, Lord,' and not do what I say?" (Luke 6:46).

The faith consists of those things most surely believed that were passed down from Jesus through the apostles and on to the saints (believers) that came in succeeding generations. This faith was a one-time event, good for all time. Now it is up to the saints to protect it and pass it on generation by generation.

The problem was that among the committed saints were some who had gained admission to the body of believers "secretly." They had not wholeheartedly given their lives to Jesus at their conversion. Apparently they came into the church with secret reservations and with ideas about the faith that were not true. Rather than growing in the grace and knowledge of Jesus Christ, they denied him as Sovereign. Jude considered himself a servant of Jesus, but these people denied the lordship of Jesus. They were unwilling to put their lives under the control of his commands and the instruction of his apostles.

These people also perverted God's intent. God shows mercy to all who will accept the salvation offered in Christ Jesus. There is freedom in Christ (John 8:31-32). But these people had used that freedom to practice sexual immorality.

Such godless people are condemned for their deeds. God condemned immorality "long ago," and that judgment has continued. God's condemnation does not lessen the danger of such behavior for immature, young Christians. Some of them had only recently been saved from the pagan society in which immoral sexual practices were normal behavior. To have similar, ungodly practices in the church was to place a stumbling block before them.

So Jude was determined to contend for the faith by writing this letter. He would give an example of a proper attitude toward ungodly behavior within the body of Christ (the church). Jude would encourage the readers on ways to build up their faith and stand firm.

❏ *Jude 5–16.* This section is the main part of Jude's letter. Here he attacks the problem of the godless by using examples from Scripture and other writings to show what God's judgment has been on similar persons. He also describes what these godless persons are like in God's view.

❏ *Jude 5–7.* These three verses provide examples drawn from the Old Testament and from the Book of Enoch. Enoch was a well-known book among Christians and Jews in the first century A.D. The book was associated with the Enoch who is mentioned in Genesis (5:21-24). He is also mentioned in Hebrews 11:5. The Book of Enoch was written in the intertestamental period and incorporates traditions about Enoch. The people to whom Jude first wrote would have been quite familiar with the stories to which he refers.

The first illustration of godless people who were destroyed is of the Israelites who perished in the wilderness after they were delivered from the slavery of Egypt. God saved them, then destroyed those who did not believe. We saw this same point in Hebrews 3:7-19. Those Israelites were rebellious against Moses and God, and that rebellion was evidence of their unbelief. In like manner the godless in the church were rebellious against Jesus and his apostles.

The second example is taken from the Book of Enoch. According to the tradition, some angels in heaven rebelled against the authority of God. This rebellion is described by Jude: "[They] did not keep their positions of authority but abandoned their own home." But Jude does not give the details of the story. The same tradition is mentioned in 2 Peter 2:4. At the Last Judgment those rebellious angels will be cast into the lake of fire (Matthew 25:41; Revelation 20:7-15).

The third example is of Sodom and Gomorrah. The story of the destruction of those cities is recorded in Genesis 19:1-28. Fire rained down from heaven on the people of Sodom and Gomorrah because of their sexual immorality. They were destroyed by a sudden and brief fire, but Jude understands that they will be consigned to the eternal fire as well.

The main point of these examples is that God will punish ungodly and immoral people. The punishment may be in this world or in eternity.

❏ *Jude 8–11.* Jude's first readers were well aware of the three examples of God's punishment on the godless. The godless men who were the problem in the church also knew those three traditions. They had not, however, seen the similarity of their deeds to those of the Israelites, the fallen angels, and the people of Sodom and Gomorrah.

Jude plainly states in verse 8 that the godless in the church "pollute their own bodies, reject authority and slander celestial beings." They polluted their bodies through improper sexual activities. They rejected the authority of Jesus by denying that he is Sovereign and Lord (verse 4). They appear also to have rejected the authority of the apostolic teaching. Instead, they established themselves as authorities based on their dreamings. Once an individual cuts loose from the authority of the revealed world of God, all sorts of wild imaginings can result.

We do not know exactly what is meant by the phrase *slander celestial beings*. Perhaps these men were making light of the glory of God. Christians are supposed to praise God and give God the glory. Instead, the godless slandered God's works.

Jude says that even Michael the archangel refrained from slandering the devil when he might have. The Bible has no story of the angel contending with the devil over the body of Moses. This tradition is from Jewish circles dating before the time of Jesus. The story was well known to Jude's first readers. We know of the story through a nonbiblical book called The Assumption of Moses.

The details of the story are not important. Clearly Jude thought that to slander is utterly unchristian, and that is why he mentions the story. To slander is to condemn with insulting or mocking words. Such rebuking is to be left to God. Yet these people in the church are guilty of slandering "whatever they do not understand."

Polluters of the body, slanderers of God, and rejecters of authority have always been condemned by God. To do these things is to bring destruction on oneself. God's punishment will come on them just as it did on Cain (Genesis 4:3-16), on Balaam (Numbers 22–24; 31:8), and on the Israelites who joined in Korah's rebellion against the authority of Moses (Numbers 16).

❏ *Jude 12–13.* In these verses Jude describes the conduct and worthless nature of the godless in the church. They are like reefs (blemishes) hidden beneath the surface of the sea, upon which an unsuspecting boat can be dashed. In the fellowship dinners they set a selfish example. They carouse with one another in sexually suggestive ways. This conduct is in contrast to the pure-minded concern for others that ought to be a part of a Christian gathering.

The godless are like clouds that teasingly offer rain to the dry, thirsty land; but they give no rain. They think themselves teachers of special revelation gotten through their perverse dreams, but their doctrine brings no new life to the church.

The godless are like trees that bear no fruit in the time of harvest. They are barren. They are uprooted—twice dead—with no connection to the life-giving soil of God's word and will.

The godless are like "wild waves of the sea," showing great activity but accomplishing nothing beneficial. Of what value to the church is their boasting and their shameless activity?

And the godless are like wandering stars (comets). As a part of the church, these people ought to be fixed lights, so the lost of the world can be guided by their light. Instead, they are traveling toward outer darkness, toward hell.

❑ *Jude 14–16.* Jude again refers to the Book of Enoch. This book has a tradition that Enoch prophesied God's judgment on the ungodly like these men in the churches of Jude's time. The "thousands upon thousands of his holy ones" means the uncounted thousands of God's angels.

Jude mentions specifically what these men are like in verse 16. Their acts are proof that they are ungodly and fit the prophetic picture of Enoch. Such activities are exactly the opposite of what is expected of those who follow Jesus.

❑ *Jude 17–23.* In this section Jude emphasizes three things. First, he reminds his readers that ungodly people would appear in the last days. This statement is similar to 2 Peter 3:2-3. What are scoffers like? Jude notes that scoffers are driven by their sinful desires. They cause division in the body of Christ by emphasizing unscriptural ideas and gathering supporters and followers. They lack evidence of possessing the Holy Spirit because they are worldly minded.

Jude, however, is writing to the faithful. He has warned them of the dangerous influence of the godless in their midst. Now he encourages the faithful to strengthen themselves in the holy faith. This way of holy faith is the opposite of walking in an ungodly way. Jude's specific recommendations are to pray in accordance with the will of the Holy Spirit, to be actively obedient in a loving relationship with God, and to look for the return of the Lord Jesus Christ. In his mercy Christ will provide eternal life to those who so wait.

By following Jude's instruction, the faithful can have a positive influence on others. Doubters can be convinced of the truth about God by a vital Christian witness. Some who might have been lost will be saved. Even those who seem to be rolling in the filth of worldliness should not be overlooked. Fear what they do; sin can be contagious. But extend a merciful witness to them.

❑ *Jude 24–25.* Jude has finished warning and encouraging the readers. He closes with a beautiful benediction. It is a gentle hint to his readers to give God the glory, for through God's power they can be saved from falling. They are made holy, without blemish, by God's power to save them through Jesus Christ our Lord. To God also is the majesty, power, and authority.

DIMENSION THREE: WHAT DOES THE BIBLE MEAN TO ME?

1. Jude urged his readers to "contend for the faith" (verse 3). How should Christians contend for the faith in our time and circumstances?

2. How big a problem to your spiritual health is the tendency to follow your own sinful desires? How big a problem is this in your church (verses 16-19)?

Made in the USA
San Bernardino, CA
11 April 2017